Cybersecurity Awareness Programs

Dedication

This book is dedicated to the unsung heroes of cybersecurity– the individuals who tirelessly work behind the scenes to protect our digital world. It is dedicated to the security
professionals who strive to make the internet a safer place, and the countless employees who, through their vigilance and commitment to security best practices, form the strongest line of defense against cyber threats. This work is a testament to their often-unseen contributions and a recognition of their critical role in maintaining digital security. It is also dedicated to those who are just beginning their journey in cybersecurity, providing them with the knowledge and tools to make a meaningful difference. Finally, this book is dedicated to the future generation of security professionals – those who will inherit the challenges and triumphs of the digital landscape, and who will continue to innovate and improve upon our collective efforts to make cyberspace safer and more secure for all. Their dedication and passion are what drives innovation and progress in the ever-evolving field of cybersecurity. May this book serve as a guidepost on their path, offering insights and strategies for building effective and sustainable cybersecurity awareness programs for years to come. The fight for a safer digital world is a continuous endeavor, and each individual contribution, no matter how small, makes a significant difference. To all those committed to this vital cause, this book is gratefully dedicated.

Preface

In today's hyper-connected world, cybersecurity threats are more prevalent and sophisticated than ever before. While technological defenses are crucial, the human element remains the weakest link in many organizations' security posture. This book is born from the realization that effective cybersecurity awareness training is not just a best practice – it's a necessity. It's no longer enough to simply install firewalls and antivirus software; we must cultivate a security-conscious culture within organizations, empowering employees to actively participate in protecting sensitive data and systems. This book aims to bridge the gap between theory and practice, providing actionable strategies and practical tools for building and implementing impactful cybersecurity awareness programs. We move beyond abstract concepts, offering a marketing-centric approach, encouraging readers to view cybersecurity awareness as an ongoing campaign – a constant engagement and dialogue with employees. This involves creatively utilizing various communication channels, from emails and posters to interactive games and e-learning modules. We underscore the importance of measurement, emphasizing Kirkpatrick's Four Levels of Evaluation to demonstrate the return on investment (ROI) of awareness initiatives. This book is designed for a diverse audience, catering to IT professionals, security managers, HR personnel, and anyone responsible for enhancing their organization's cybersecurity readiness. Whether you're a seasoned cybersecurity expert or a newcomer to the field, you'll find practical guidance, templates, examples, and best practices to create a more secure and resilient organization. The ultimate goal is to empower readers to foster a culture of security, transforming employees from potential vulnerabilities into active participants in protecting their organization's valuable assets. The journey towards a more secure digital future starts with raising awareness – and this book is designed to be your essential guide on that journey. It is a practical, engaging resource offering a blend of strategic insights and actionable steps, making it indispensable for anyone invested in building a robust and effective cybersecurity awareness program.

Introduction

The digital landscape is constantly evolving, with new threats and vulnerabilities emerging daily. While technological solutions are essential to a robust cybersecurity strategy, they are only part of the equation. The human element remains a critical factor, and often the most vulnerable point of attack. This book provides a comprehensive guide to building and implementing effective cybersecurity awareness programs, focusing on practical strategies and actionable steps to engage employees and foster a security-conscious culture. We go beyond theoretical discussions, offering a hands-on approach that utilizes proven methods and techniques to maximize impact. This includes leveraging various communication channels – email campaigns, engaging posters, interactive games, and compelling e-learning modules – to ensure a high level of employee participation and comprehension. The focus is on creating a program that resonates with employees, converting potential vulnerabilities into active participants in protecting their organization's assets. This involves understanding diverse learning styles, simplifying complex concepts, and measuring the effectiveness of the program using established frameworks such as Kirkpatrick's Four Levels of Evaluation. A key aspect of this book is its emphasis on demonstrating return on investment (ROI). We provide practical strategies for collecting data, analyzing results, and presenting the effectiveness of the awareness program to stakeholders. This allows readers to justify budget requests and secure continued support for their security initiatives. The book is structured to be accessible to a broad audience, from IT professionals and security managers to HR personnel and those with limited technical backgrounds. It provides clear, concise explanations, real-world examples, and practical templates, making it a valuable resource for anyone involved in developing and implementing a successful cybersecurity awareness program. Ultimately, this book aims to equip readers with the knowledge and tools necessary to build a culture of security within their organization, significantly reducing the risk of cyberattacks and fostering a stronger overall security posture. The path to enhanced cybersecurity isn't merely about technology; it's about people. This book provides the framework for engaging those people effectively.

Defining Cybersecurity Awareness and its Importance

Cybersecurity awareness is not merely a buzzword; it's the bedrock upon which a robust organizational security posture is built. In today's interconnected world, where digital threats loom large and sophisticated attacks become increasingly commonplace, the human element remains the weakest link in the chain. This is not to diminish the importance of technological safeguards, firewalls, intrusion detection systems, and the like. Rather, it emphasizes the crucial role that informed and vigilant employees play in preventing and mitigating cyber risks. A robust cybersecurity awareness program acts as a crucial first line of defense, transforming potentially vulnerable individuals into active participants in the organization's security strategy.

The importance of cybersecurity awareness stems from the simple fact that human error is often the root cause of many security breaches. Phishing scams, social engineering attacks, and accidental data leaks are all testaments to this reality. A single click on a malicious link, an unsuspecting response to a fraudulent email, or a moment of carelessness in handling sensitive data can have catastrophic consequences, leading to data breaches, financial losses, reputational damage, and even legal ramifications. Therefore, investing in a comprehensive cybersecurity awareness program is not just a matter of compliance; it's a strategic imperative for ensuring business continuity and protecting the organization's valuable assets.

The evolving threat landscape further underscores the critical need for continuous cybersecurity awareness. Cybercriminals are constantly refining their techniques, developing new and more sophisticated attack vectors. From ransomware attacks targeting critical infrastructure to sophisticated phishing campaigns designed to bypass even the most robust security measures, the threats are multifaceted and ever-changing. To effectively counter these threats, organizations must cultivate a culture of vigilance and proactive security awareness amongst their employees. This requires more than just a one-time training session; it demands a continuous cycle of learning, reinforcement, and adaptation.

Consider the following scenarios to illustrate the potential impact of inadequate cybersecurity awareness:

Scenario 1: The Phishing Attack:
An employee receives a seemingly legitimate email, ostensibly from their bank, requesting them to update their account details. Without verifying the sender's address or scrutinizing the email's content, the employee clicks the link and unknowingly provides their login credentials to a malicious actor. The result? A compromised bank account, financial loss for the individual, and a potential breach of sensitive organizational data if the employee accesses corporate systems through the compromised account.

Scenario 2: The Social Engineering Scam:
A cunning social engineer, posing as a trusted IT professional, calls an employee, claiming to require immediate access to their computer to resolve a critical system issue. Without verifying the caller's identity, the employee grants access, unknowingly allowing the attacker to install malware and gain control of their system. The consequence? A potential malware infection that could compromise the entire network, leading to data breaches, system downtime, and significant financial losses.

Scenario 3: The Accidental Data Leak:
An employee inadvertently shares sensitive customer data via an
unencrypted email or posts confidential information on an unsecured social media platform. The consequences can range from hefty fines due to non-compliance with data privacy regulations to irreparable damage to the organization's reputation and trust amongst its customers.

These examples underscore the devastating consequences of human error in cybersecurity. A proactive cybersecurity awareness program aims to mitigate such risks by educating employees about common threats, best practices for secure computing, and the importance of reporting suspicious activity. By empowering employees with the knowledge and skills to recognize and respond to potential threats, organizations can significantly reduce their vulnerability to cyberattacks.

The effectiveness of a cybersecurity awareness program lies not only in its content but also in its delivery and engagement. A well-designed program will leverage various methods to reach and resonate with employees, fostering a culture of security and responsibility. This may involve a combination of methods, including interactive training sessions, e-learning modules, gamification techniques, phishing simulations, and regular communication campaigns. The program should be tailored to the specific needs and technical expertise of the audience, using clear, concise language and avoiding overly technical jargon. The goal is not to overwhelm employees with technical details but to empower them with the knowledge and confidence to navigate the digital landscape safely.

A successful cybersecurity awareness program is not a one-size-fits-all solution. It requires careful planning, implementation, and continuous evaluation. It needs to be regularly updated to reflect the evolving threat landscape and adapt to the changing needs of the organization. Crucially, it must be closely aligned with the organization's overall security strategy, integrating seamlessly with other security measures to form a comprehensive and robust defense against cyber threats. Ignoring the human element is a dangerous oversight. Investing in a comprehensive cybersecurity awareness program is not just a cost; it's an investment in the organization's future, safeguarding its valuable assets and ensuring its long-term viability. The ultimate goal is to foster a security-conscious culture, where employees are empowered to actively participate in protecting the organization from cyber risks. This shared responsibility forms the cornerstone of a robust and effective cybersecurity defense strategy.

Beyond the immediate benefits of reducing the risk of cyberattacks, a well-implemented cybersecurity awareness program offers a multitude of additional advantages. These include:

Improved Compliance:
A strong awareness program demonstrates due diligence and helps organizations meet compliance requirements related to data privacy regulations like GDPR, CCPA, and others. This reduces the risk of hefty fines and legal repercussions resulting from data breaches.

Enhanced Productivity:
By reducing the time lost due to security incidents, such as malware infections or phishing attacks, a robust awareness program contributes to improved overall productivity. Employees are less likely to be sidetracked by security issues, allowing them to focus on their core responsibilities.

Strengthened Reputation:
Demonstrating a proactive approach to cybersecurity enhances the organization's

reputation and builds trust with customers, partners, and stakeholders. This can lead to a competitive advantage in the marketplace.

Cost Savings:
While the initial investment in a cybersecurity awareness program may seem significant, the long-term cost savings resulting from the prevention of security incidents and reduced remediation efforts are substantial. The financial benefits of preventing a major data breach, for example, often outweigh the cost of the program many times over.

Increased Employee Engagement:
A well-designed program can improve employee engagement by making them feel more involved in the organization's security efforts. This fosters a sense of ownership and responsibility for protecting the company's assets.

In conclusion, defining cybersecurity awareness is synonymous with defining proactive risk management within the digital realm. It's not merely about ticking boxes or fulfilling regulatory requirements. It's about cultivating a security-conscious culture where every individual within the organization understands their role in mitigating cybersecurity threats. Investing in a comprehensive cybersecurity awareness program is an investment in the future of the organization, one that yields significant returns in terms of reduced risk, enhanced compliance, improved productivity, and a stronger overall security posture. The proactive, continuous approach to cybersecurity awareness is no longer a luxury; it's a necessity in today's increasingly complex and dangerous digital landscape.

Assessing Current Organizational Vulnerabilities

Assessing an organization's existing cybersecurity awareness level is the crucial first step in building an effective program. Ignoring this vital assessment phase leads to generic, ineffective training that fails to address specific vulnerabilities. A targeted approach, however, requires a thorough understanding of the current state of awareness within the organization. This involves a multi-pronged strategy encompassing vulnerability assessments, employee surveys, and detailed analysis of phishing simulation results. These combined methods paint a comprehensive picture, revealing weaknesses and informing the design of a truly effective awareness program.

Vulnerability assessments, often overlooked in the context of cybersecurity awareness, provide a crucial baseline. These assessments aren't solely focused on technical infrastructure; they extend to the human element, identifying potential weaknesses in employee understanding and behavior. Traditional vulnerability scans focus on software, network configurations, and other technical aspects, but for a comprehensive understanding, you need to move beyond the technical and consider the people. Consider, for example, a scenario where a company's vulnerability scanner identifies outdated software on employee workstations. While fixing the software is crucial, the assessment should also consider whether employees understand the risks associated with running outdated software and whether they report such issues proactively. The vulnerability assessment in this context should include a review of existing security policies, employee training materials, and even informal communication channels to gauge the extent of employee understanding. Are these policies readily accessible? Are they clearly written and easily understood by employees across all levels of technical expertise? This deeper dive into the "human vulnerabilities" allows for a more targeted approach to awareness training. For instance, you might find that the company has a strong technical infrastructure but lacks employee awareness of social engineering tactics, leaving them susceptible to phishing attacks.

Employee surveys are another powerful tool in assessing the current state of cybersecurity awareness. These surveys should not be generic questionnaires; instead, they should be carefully designed to uncover specific knowledge gaps and behavioral patterns. The questions should be tailored to the organization's specific context, industry, and the types of threats they face. Open-ended questions can be particularly valuable in uncovering unexpected insights and perspectives. For instance, instead of asking "Do you know what phishing is?", consider asking "Describe a situation where you might encounter a phishing attempt." This type of question encourages more thoughtful and nuanced responses, revealing both understanding and potential blind spots. The survey should also explore employees' comfort levels in reporting security incidents, their understanding of the company's security policies, and their knowledge of common threats such as malware, ransomware, and social engineering. Furthermore, it's essential to ensure anonymity to encourage honest and candid responses. Data from the survey needs to be thoroughly analyzed, looking for trends and patterns that indicate specific areas of weakness. For example, if a significant number of respondents demonstrate a lack of understanding concerning password security, this clearly identifies a focus area for the awareness program.

Phishing simulations are an invaluable method for assessing the effectiveness of existing awareness programs and identifying vulnerabilities in employee behavior. These simulations present realistic scenarios mimicking actual phishing attempts, allowing you to evaluate how employees respond. The results offer quantifiable data on click-through rates, the number of employees who fell for the simulation, and the types of phishing tactics most effective against your workforce. For example, if a significant portion of employees click on links in emails purporting to be from internal IT staff requesting login credentials, this clearly points to a need for increased awareness training on internal phishing attempts. Similarly, if many employees fall for a specific type of phishing tactic, such as a sense of urgency or a fraudulent prize, that type of tactic can be incorporated into targeted training modules. It's important to use diverse types of phishing attempts to provide a broader picture, reflecting the ever-evolving landscape of cyber threats. The detailed analysis of simulation results must go beyond simply measuring the success or failure rate. It should delve into the reasons why employees fell for the simulation. Was it due to a lack of knowledge, a lack of attention, or a combination of factors? Post-simulation interviews can provide valuable qualitative data to supplement the quantitative findings from the simulation. Understanding the reasons behind the failures allows for the creation of tailored training that addresses the root causes of vulnerability.

Once the data from vulnerability assessments, employee surveys, and phishing simulations has been collected, the next step is meticulous analysis and interpretation. This involves consolidating the findings from all three methods to create a comprehensive profile of the organization's cybersecurity awareness strengths and weaknesses. For example, if the vulnerability assessment highlights outdated software, the employee survey reveals low awareness of patching procedures, and the phishing simulation demonstrates a high susceptibility to spear-phishing attacks, this indicates a clear need for training on software updates, patching procedures, and recognizing sophisticated phishing attempts. The analysis should also consider the organizational context. Factors like industry regulations, the sensitivity of the data handled by the organization, and the existing technological infrastructure should all be taken into account. For example, a healthcare organization handling sensitive patient data would require a far more rigorous awareness program than a small retail business.

Creating a targeted awareness program based on these findings requires a nuanced understanding of the organization's specific vulnerabilities. The program should not be a generic, one-size-fits-all approach. Instead, it should directly address the specific weaknesses identified through the assessment process. This might involve creating targeted training modules focused on specific threats, developing customized phishing simulations to address identified vulnerabilities, or implementing improved communication channels to ensure that security policies and updates are effectively disseminated. The chosen methods of delivery should also consider the preferences and learning styles of the employees, ranging from interactive e-learning modules and engaging videos to instructor-led classroom sessions and gamified training. For example, employees who are visually oriented might benefit from videos and infographics, whereas employees who prefer hands-on learning might find gamified training or simulations more effective. Finally, the program should include a robust mechanism for measuring its effectiveness. This might involve repeating the phishing simulations, conducting follow-up surveys, or monitoring incident reports to assess the impact of the training on employee behavior and the organization's overall security posture. Continuous monitoring and evaluation are critical to ensuring the ongoing effectiveness of the awareness program and its ability to adapt to the evolving threat landscape. By understanding the nuances of an organization's specific vulnerabilities and tailoring the awareness program accordingly, organizations can significantly reduce their risk of cyberattacks and build a stronger security posture.

The process of assessing current organizational vulnerabilities extends beyond a single snapshot in time. It should be viewed as an ongoing process of continuous improvement and adaptation. Regular updates to the vulnerability assessments, employee surveys, and phishing simulations provide a dynamic view of the evolving security awareness landscape within the organization. This iterative approach allows the organization to respond effectively to emerging threats and adapt its awareness program to meet the ever-changing needs of the digital environment. The ongoing assessment, analysis, and adaptation form a continuous feedback loop. This loop helps refine the training content and delivery methods, making them more relevant and engaging for employees, ultimately increasing the effectiveness of the cybersecurity awareness program. Regularly reviewing the data allows the organization to proactively identify and address new vulnerabilities before they can be exploited by malicious actors. It's also crucial to communicate the results of these assessments and the corresponding program adaptations to employees. This transparency builds trust and demonstrates a commitment to enhancing the organization's overall security posture.

Finally, it's important to remember that the goal of a cybersecurity awareness program is not just to check a box or fulfill regulatory requirements. It's about fostering a culture of security where employees feel empowered and responsible for protecting the organization's assets. By integrating cybersecurity awareness into the fabric of the organization's culture, it ceases to be a separate initiative and instead becomes an integral part of daily operations. This cultural shift is best achieved through consistent reinforcement, clear communication, and employee engagement. Regular reminders, incentives for reporting incidents, and recognition of employees who demonstrate strong security practices all contribute to building a robust security culture. This continuous effort is far more effective than a one-off training session and ultimately contributes to a much lower risk profile for the organization. The iterative process of assessment, adaptation, and ongoing reinforcement is essential to ensuring the long-term success of any cybersecurity awareness program. Investing in these continuous improvements is an investment in the organization's resilience against cyber threats and its overall success in the digital age.

Legal and Regulatory Compliance Considerations

Building a comprehensive cybersecurity awareness program isn't simply a matter of ticking boxes; it's a critical component of maintaining legal and regulatory compliance. The increasing sophistication of cyberattacks and the growing volume of sensitive data necessitate a proactive and demonstrably effective approach to security. Failure to adequately protect this data can lead to significant financial penalties, reputational damage, and even criminal prosecution. Understanding the legal landscape and how a robust awareness program contributes to compliance is therefore paramount.

The legal ramifications of data breaches vary depending on the jurisdiction and the nature of the breach. However, the consequences are consistently severe. Consider the General Data Protection Regulation (GDPR) in the European Union, a landmark piece of legislation that imposes stringent requirements on organizations handling personal data. GDPR stipulates significant fines for non-compliance, potentially reaching up to €20 million or 4% of annual global turnover – whichever is greater. This highlights the high stakes involved and the importance of a meticulously planned and executed cybersecurity awareness program.

Similarly, the California Consumer Privacy Act (CCPA) in the United States grants California residents specific rights regarding their personal data, including the right to access, delete, and opt-out of the sale of their data. Breaches of CCPA can result in substantial penalties, further emphasizing the need for proactive measures to prevent data breaches and ensure compliance. Other state-level regulations and sector-specific laws add further layers of complexity. The Health

Insurance Portability and Accountability Act (HIPAA) in the US, for instance, imposes strict regulations on the protection of protected health information (PHI), with severe penalties for non-compliance. The Payment Card Industry Data Security Standard (PCI DSS) sets standards for organizations handling credit card information, demanding rigorous security protocols and regular audits.

Navigating this complex legal landscape requires a multi-faceted strategy, and a strong cybersecurity awareness program is a cornerstone of that strategy. A well-designed program doesn't just meet the minimum requirements of compliance; it actively fosters a culture of security throughout the organization. This culture translates to employees who understand the importance of data protection, who are vigilant about potential threats, and who proactively report suspicious activity. This proactive approach significantly reduces the likelihood of breaches and minimizes the potential impact should a breach occur.

Demonstrating due diligence is crucial in minimizing legal exposure. This involves not only implementing robust technical security measures but also meticulously documenting the cybersecurity awareness program. This documentation should clearly outline the program's objectives, training materials, methods of delivery, and methods for measuring effectiveness. Regular audits of the program are essential to ensure that it remains effective and up-to-date with evolving threats and legal requirements. This documentation serves as concrete evidence of the organization's commitment to data protection and can be invaluable in mitigating legal risks in the event of a breach. In essence, a well-documented program demonstrates a proactive and responsible approach to security, potentially lessening the severity of penalties in the case of a security incident.

The effectiveness of a cybersecurity awareness program extends beyond simply complying with regulations. It impacts the organization's overall risk profile. A culture of security fosters proactive reporting of suspicious activity, reducing the window of vulnerability during a potential attack. Prompt detection and response are critical in minimizing the impact of a breach and limiting the amount of data compromised. A well-trained workforce is less likely to fall victim to phishing attacks, ransomware, and other common cyber threats, thereby significantly reducing the risk of data breaches and the associated legal and financial consequences.

Furthermore, the program's impact extends to the organization's reputation. In today's interconnected world, a data breach can severely damage an organization's reputation, leading to loss of customer trust and potential financial losses. Demonstrating a commitment to cybersecurity through a robust awareness program can mitigate this risk. A reputation for strong data protection practices can be a significant competitive advantage, while a history of data breaches can have lasting negative consequences.

The development of a comprehensive cybersecurity awareness program that addresses legal and regulatory compliance requires careful planning and execution. A key element is understanding the specific regulations and laws that apply to the organization. This may involve consulting with legal counsel to ensure that the program fully addresses all relevant requirements. The program should be tailored to the specific needs of the organization, taking into account the nature of the data handled, the size and structure of the organization, and the specific types of threats it faces.

Regular updates and revisions are essential to ensure that the program remains effective. The threat landscape is constantly evolving, with new threats emerging regularly. The program should be regularly reviewed and updated to address these new threats, and to incorporate lessons learned from past incidents or industry best practices. This continuous improvement process is crucial in maintaining a strong security posture and ensuring ongoing compliance.

The program should also be designed to be engaging and effective. Employees are more likely to take the program seriously if it is presented in an engaging and relevant manner. This may involve the use of interactive training modules, gamification, and other techniques to keep employees interested and motivated. Regular assessments and feedback mechanisms can help to measure the effectiveness of the program and identify areas for improvement.

Legal and regulatory compliance is not a static endpoint but a continuous process. Ongoing monitoring, adaptation, and improvement are crucial to stay abreast of evolving regulations and emerging threats. A successful cybersecurity awareness program is not a one-time event, but rather an ongoing commitment to security, requiring continuous investment in training, resources, and employee engagement. The cost of non-compliance far outweighs the investment required to implement a robust program, and the benefits—reduced risk, enhanced reputation, and legal protection—are significant. Investing in a proactive and comprehensive cybersecurity awareness program is not merely a matter of compliance; it's an investment in the long-term sustainability and success of the organization. By embracing a culture of security and continuous improvement, organizations can significantly mitigate their risk and protect their valuable data in the face of ever-evolving cyber threats. This approach not only fulfills legal obligations but also strengthens the organization's resilience, ensuring its ability to thrive in the increasingly digital world. The importance of a robust cybersecurity awareness program cannot be overstated; it's a critical investment in the future of the organization.

Establishing Measurable Goals and Objectives

Establishing a robust cybersecurity awareness program requires more than simply delivering training; it demands a strategic approach underpinned by clearly defined goals and objectives. Without measurable targets, it becomes impossible to assess the program's effectiveness, demonstrate return on investment (ROI), and justify continued investment. This section will guide you through the process of defining SMART goals—Specific, Measurable, Achievable, Relevant, and Time-bound—ensuring your program's impact is demonstrable and aligns with overall organizational objectives.

The first step is to clearly define your program's overarching goals. What are you hoping to achieve? Are you aiming to reduce phishing attacks? Improve password hygiene? Enhance employee understanding of social engineering tactics? These broad goals need to be translated into specific, measurable objectives. Instead of aiming for "improved security awareness," a SMART objective might be: "Reduce successful phishing attacks by 25% within six months." This objective is specific, quantifiable, and has a clear timeframe.

This level of specificity is crucial for several reasons. First, it provides a clear benchmark against which to measure success. Second, it allows for accurate tracking of progress, enabling timely adjustments to the program if necessary. Third, it provides concrete evidence of the program's value to stakeholders, demonstrating a tangible return on the investment in time, resources, and personnel.

When defining measurable objectives, it's important to consider key performance indicators (KPIs). KPIs are quantifiable metrics that provide insights into the effectiveness of your program. Examples of relevant KPIs include:

Phishing Simulation Success Rate:

This KPI measures the percentage of employees who successfully identify and report phishing attempts during simulated attacks. A decreasing success rate indicates an improvement in employee awareness and ability to recognize and respond to phishing threats. Tracking this metric over time demonstrates the program's direct impact on reducing the likelihood of successful phishing attacks.

Security Awareness Training Completion Rate:

This KPI tracks the percentage of employees who complete the required security awareness training within a given timeframe. A high completion rate suggests good engagement and program accessibility. However, a high completion rate alone doesn't guarantee effectiveness; it should be coupled with other KPIs to ensure comprehensive evaluation. For example, a high completion rate combined with a low phishing simulation success rate would suggest that the training is ineffective and needs revision.

Number of Security Incidents Reported:

This KPI measures the number of security incidents reported by employees. An increase in reported incidents, particularly those related to phishing attempts or suspicious activity, may initially seem negative, but it actually indicates increased employee awareness and a willingness to report potential threats. This proactive reporting is critical for early threat detection and mitigation, thus contributing significantly to overall organizational security.

Password Strength:

Analyzing password complexity and adherence to password policies provides insights into employee understanding and compliance with password security guidelines. A higher average password strength score demonstrates the effectiveness of training and reinforcement regarding password hygiene. Tools and dashboards are readily available to monitor this KPI, providing valuable data to assess program impact.

Time to Respond to Security Incidents:
This KPI
measures the time it takes employees to report and respond to security incidents. A decrease in response time highlights improved employee awareness and preparedness, enabling quicker mitigation of threats. This is particularly relevant for incidents such as data breaches or malware infections, where swift action is crucial to minimize damage.

Employee Knowledge Scores:
Pre- and post-training
assessments can measure changes in employee knowledge and understanding of key cybersecurity concepts. This KPI provides direct evidence of the effectiveness of the training content and its impact on employee awareness. A significant increase in post-training scores indicates successful knowledge transfer and skill development.

The choice of KPIs will depend on the specific goals of your program and the resources available for monitoring and measurement. It's crucial to select KPIs that are relevant, easily measurable, and align with your overall objectives. Avoid selecting too many KPIs, as this can lead to analysis paralysis. Focus on a few key metrics that provide the most valuable insights into the program's effectiveness.

In addition to selecting relevant KPIs, it's crucial to establish a baseline. Before implementing your cybersecurity awareness program, measure your current performance using your chosen KPIs. This baseline provides a point of comparison against which to track future progress and demonstrate the program's impact. For example, if your baseline phishing simulation success rate is 70%, a successful program should demonstrate a significant reduction in this rate over time.

Once your goals and KPIs are established, you need to consider how you will collect and analyze data. This might involve using specialized security awareness training platforms, utilizing survey tools, or implementing data logging mechanisms within your existing security infrastructure. The chosen methods should be efficient and reliable, allowing for accurate and consistent data collection.

The success of a cybersecurity awareness program hinges on its ability to be continuously improved and adapted based on data-driven insights. Regularly reviewing your KPIs and analyzing the data they provide allows you to identify areas for improvement and make adjustments to your program as needed. This iterative approach ensures the program remains relevant, effective, and aligned with the ever-evolving threat landscape.

For example, if the data reveals a consistent failure to identify a particular type of phishing attack, you can adapt your training program to include more detailed instruction on recognizing that specific type of threat. This data-driven approach ensures that your resources are focused on addressing the most critical weaknesses in your organization's security posture.

Finally, remember to communicate the program's success (or areas needing improvement) to relevant stakeholders. This involves presenting the data collected from your KPIs in a clear and concise manner, demonstrating the return on investment (ROI) and the value of the cybersecurity awareness program to the organization. This transparency fosters ongoing support and ensures the program continues to receive the necessary resources to maintain its effectiveness. Regular reporting, including visual representations of data trends, such as graphs and charts, can greatly enhance understanding and provide compelling evidence of the program's success. This consistent communication builds trust and ensures that the cybersecurity awareness program is viewed as a valuable asset within the organization, rather than just another compliance exercise. Ultimately, by setting SMART goals, carefully selecting KPIs, and diligently tracking progress, you can transform your cybersecurity awareness program from a compliance obligation into a powerful instrument for enhancing organizational security and demonstrating a tangible return on investment.

Budgeting and Resource Allocation for a Successful Program

Building a successful cybersecurity awareness program requires a significant investment, not just in terms of time and effort, but also financially. Securing the necessary budget and strategically allocating resources is critical to the program's success. This section will guide you through the process of developing a realistic budget, identifying cost-effective strategies, and justifying the investment to stakeholders.

The first step is a thorough needs assessment. This involves identifying the specific training requirements of your organization, considering factors such as employee roles, technical expertise, and the types of threats your organization faces. This analysis will inform the scope and content of your program, directly impacting the resources you'll need. For example, a large multinational corporation with a diverse workforce and complex IT infrastructure will have vastly different needs compared to a small, locally-owned business. The former might require extensive e-learning modules, sophisticated phishing simulations, and specialized training for different departments, while the latter might benefit from a simpler, more focused approach using a combination of short, engaging videos and regular email reminders.

Once you've determined the specific training needs, you can begin to estimate the costs involved. These costs can be broadly categorized into several areas:

1. Training Materials and Content Development:
This includes the cost of developing or purchasing e-learning

modules, creating engaging videos, designing presentations, printing brochures and posters, and procuring any necessary hardware or software. Consider the cost of external consultants or designers to ensure your materials are both informative and engaging. Open-source resources can significantly reduce costs, but remember that the quality and effectiveness may vary, so thorough vetting is crucial. Furthermore, consider the ongoing costs associated with updating training materials to reflect changes in threat landscapes and security best practices. Regularly updating your materials ensures employees receive current, relevant information, maximizing the effectiveness of the training program.

2. Software and Technology:
You'll need to budget for software to deliver training, track employee progress, and manage the program. This could include Learning
Management Systems (LMS), phishing simulation platforms, and security awareness training platforms. The choice of software will depend on your organization's size, budget, and specific needs. Some LMS platforms offer free versions with limited functionality, but for larger organizations, a premium subscription offering advanced features like detailed reporting and analytics will be necessary. Additionally, factor in potential costs for software licenses and any required upgrades or maintenance. The investment in robust software can streamline the program's administration and provide valuable insights into its effectiveness.

3. Personnel Costs:
This is arguably the most significant expense for many organizations. Consider the costs
associated with internal staff involved in the program's design, development, delivery, and maintenance. If your program is extensive, you might need to dedicate a full-time employee to manage it. Alternatively, you may opt for outsourcing some tasks or leveraging existing IT staff's

expertise. Remember to calculate the time involved in planning, creating content, delivering training, managing the LMS, tracking progress, and generating reports. Accurate estimation of personnel costs is critical for a realistic budget.

4. External Trainers and Consultants:

Depending on the scope of your program and the organization's internal
expertise, you may require the services of external trainers or consultants. These experts can provide specialized training on advanced topics, design engaging training materials, or conduct assessments to evaluate the program's effectiveness. The cost of external expertise can vary significantly based on experience, expertise, and the duration of their involvement.

5. Campaign and Marketing Materials:

A robust
cybersecurity awareness program doesn't exist in a vacuum. It needs to be actively promoted to employees to ensure maximum participation and engagement. This means investing in creative marketing materials: eye-catching posters, informative emails, engaging social media posts, and potentially even interactive games or competitions. These costs can vary greatly depending on your chosen methods and the scale of your campaign. A well-designed campaign ensures that the message reaches the right audience in the right way, making the training more relevant and impactful.

6. Measurement and Evaluation:

It's crucial to invest in tools and resources to measure the program's effectiveness.
This may involve using surveys, quizzes, or phishing simulations to assess employee knowledge and behavior. Budget for the time involved in analyzing the collected data and preparing reports demonstrating the return on investment (ROI). Data-driven insights allow you to fine-tune your program, improve its impact, and justify continued investment.

7. Contingency Planning:

Always include a contingency fund in your budget. Unforeseen issues may arise, such as the need for additional training materials, unexpected software costs, or the need for external support. A contingency fund allows you to handle these issues without disrupting the program's progress. This is particularly important for long-term programs.

Once you've estimated the costs in each area, you can consolidate these into a comprehensive budget. This budget should be clearly presented to stakeholders, highlighting the value and the return on investment (ROI) of a successful cybersecurity awareness program. Demonstrate how investing in a strong program will reduce the risk of security incidents, protecting sensitive data, and minimizing potential financial losses. You can illustrate the potential cost of a data breach versus the cost of a well-executed awareness program to effectively showcase the cost-benefit analysis. Quantify the potential savings resulting from reduced incidents and improved employee behavior. Include visual representations of your data, such as charts and graphs, to ensure clear communication of the program's value.

Remember to focus on the long-term benefits. A well-designed and well-funded cybersecurity awareness program is not merely a one-time expense but an ongoing investment that continuously protects the organization from evolving cyber threats. By highlighting these long-term benefits, you can build a strong case for obtaining the necessary resources and demonstrating the enduring value of the program. Demonstrate how a proactive and continuously evolving awareness program contributes to a more secure and resilient organization, thereby protecting its reputation, customer trust, and long-term financial stability.

Finally, don't be afraid to explore cost-effective solutions. This might involve leveraging free or open-source resources, partnering with other organizations to share resources, or utilizing internal expertise instead of hiring external consultants. Creative resource allocation can significantly reduce the overall cost without compromising the program's effectiveness. The key is to find a balance between investing enough to create a high-impact program and maintaining fiscal responsibility. By carefully planning your budget, justifying the investment, and strategically allocating your resources, you can build a cybersecurity awareness program that is both effective and sustainable.

Crafting Compelling Training Materials

Crafting compelling cybersecurity awareness training materials is paramount to the success of any program. Simply presenting information isn't enough; you need to capture your audience's attention and make the learning experience both engaging and memorable. This requires a deep understanding of your audience's needs, learning styles, and existing knowledge levels. Remember, your goal isn't just to deliver information; it's to instill a culture of security and empower employees to become active participants in protecting your organization.

One of the first steps is to analyze your audience. This isn't a one-size-fits-all approach. You'll likely have diverse groups within your organization, each requiring a tailored approach. Consider the following factors:

Technical Proficiency:
Do your employees possess a strong technical background, or are they largely non-technical? Your language and examples need to reflect this. For highly technical audiences, you can use more specialized terminology and delve deeper into technical details. For non-technical audiences, stick to plain language, utilize analogies, and focus on the practical implications of security risks. Avoid jargon that will confuse or alienate them.

Learning Styles:
People learn in different ways. Some are visual learners who respond well to images, videos, and infographics. Others are auditory learners who prefer audio explanations, discussions, and presentations. Kinesthetic learners benefit from hands-on activities and simulations. A truly effective training program incorporates diverse methods to cater to all learning styles.

Existing Knowledge:
Gauge your audience's pre-existing understanding of cybersecurity. A comprehensive needs assessment (which we'll cover in greater detail later) can help identify knowledge gaps and tailor your materials to address these areas specifically. Begin with a review of fundamental concepts before moving on to more complex subjects. Avoid overwhelming your audience with too much information at once.

Simplifying Complex Topics:
Cybersecurity can be a daunting field, full of complex terminology and technical details. Your challenge is to present this information in an easily digestible manner. Here are some effective strategies:

Use Analogies and Real-world Examples:
Relate cybersecurity concepts to everyday situations your employees can understand. For instance, explain phishing attacks by comparing them to receiving a suspicious email from someone claiming to be a bank representative, requesting personal information. Explain firewalls by comparing them to the physical security systems at your office building.

Break Down Complex Information into Smaller Chunks:
Avoid overwhelming your audience with dense paragraphs of information. Break down complex topics into smaller, manageable sections. Use headings, subheadings, bullet points, and visuals to improve readability and comprehension.

Focus on Practical Applications:
Instead of focusing solely on theoretical concepts, emphasize the practical implications of cybersecurity threats. Show your audience how these threats affect their daily work and the potential consequences of neglecting security measures.

Storytelling:
Employ narratives to illustrate important concepts. A compelling story can make complex ideas more engaging and easier to remember. Think about describing a data breach and its impact on a company or an individual, thus driving home the importance of security practices.

Visuals are Key:
Our brains process visual information much faster than text. Visuals significantly enhance engagement and knowledge retention. Consider these options:

Infographics:
Infographics are visually appealing and effective for summarizing complex information concisely. They break down complicated topics into easy-to-understand chunks, using visuals, icons, and minimal text.

Videos and Animations:
Short, engaging videos and animations can bring cybersecurity concepts to life. They can demonstrate attacks in action or explain technical processes in a visually intuitive way.

Illustrations and Diagrams:
Simple illustrations and diagrams can significantly improve understanding of complex concepts. For example, a diagram of a network architecture can help employees visualize how security measures protect different parts of their organization's infrastructure.

Interactive Elements:
Interactive elements boost engagement and make the learning process more active. Consider using quizzes, polls, and simulations to encourage active participation and assess understanding.

Incorporating Interactive Elements:
Passive learning is far less effective than active learning. Interactive elements

significantly enhance engagement and knowledge retention. Here are some ideas:

Interactive Quizzes and Assessments:
Include quizzes at the end of each module to test comprehension and identify knowledge gaps. These assessments should be integrated into the learning experience, not just serve as an afterthought. Make them fun and challenging, not punitive.

Simulations:
Phishing simulations are a powerful tool for training employees to recognize and report suspicious emails. These simulations can realistically replicate real-world phishing attacks, helping employees develop skills in identifying and responding to these threats. Consider other simulations that explore different attack vectors, like social engineering or malware.

Scenario-based Exercises:
Present employees with realistic cybersecurity scenarios and ask them to make decisions based on their understanding of security best practices. This hands-on approach promotes critical thinking and problem-solving skills.

Games and Gamification:
Gamification can transform learning into a fun and competitive experience. Incorporate points systems, leaderboards, badges, and rewards to motivate employees and encourage active participation. Points-based systems motivate employees to complete modules, answer quizzes correctly, and participate in interactive sessions.

Accessibility and Inclusivity:
When designing your materials, it's crucial to ensure they are accessible to all employees, regardless of their abilities or learning styles.
Consider the following:

Accessibility Standards:
Adhere to accessibility standards like WCAG (Web Content Accessibility Guidelines) to make your materials usable for individuals with disabilities. This includes providing alternative text for images, ensuring sufficient color contrast, and using keyboard navigation.

Multilingual Support:
If your workforce speaks multiple languages, provide training materials in those languages to ensure everyone can access the information.

Diverse Representations:
Use diverse images and scenarios in your training materials to reflect the diversity of your workforce. This inclusivity helps everyone feel seen and included in the learning process.

Review and Revision:
Once you've created your training materials, don't consider them set in stone. Regularly review and revise your materials based on feedback from employees and the results of your training assessments. Cybersecurity threats and best practices constantly evolve, so your training materials should evolve alongside them. This iterative process ensures your program remains effective and current.

By implementing these strategies, you'll create engaging and effective cybersecurity awareness training materials that resonate with your employees, foster a culture of security, and ultimately protect your organization from cyber threats. Remember, a well-designed training program is an investment, not an expense. The effort you put into creating compelling materials will pay off in the form of a more secure and resilient organization.

Developing Effective Elearning Modules

Building effective e-learning modules requires a strategic approach that goes beyond simply uploading PowerPoint slides. The goal is to create an interactive and engaging learning experience that resonates with employees and fosters a culture of security. This necessitates careful consideration of several key aspects: design, content delivery, assessment, accessibility, and the choice of learning platform.

Let's start with
design
. The visual appeal of your e-learning module significantly impacts its effectiveness. Avoid cluttered interfaces and overwhelming amounts of text. Use a consistent visual style guide, incorporating your company's branding where appropriate. Employ high-quality images, videos, and animations to break up large blocks of text and maintain viewer engagement. Consider using a storytelling approach; weaving cybersecurity principles into narratives makes the information more relatable and memorable. Remember the importance of white space; giving the eye room to breathe improves readability and comprehension. Intuitive navigation is crucial; learners should easily move through the module without frustration. Clear, concise instructions and a logical flow are essential for a positive user experience. A well-structured module guides the learner efficiently through the material, ensuring key concepts are absorbed effectively. Think about incorporating interactive elements like quizzes, polls, and branching scenarios. These not only enhance engagement but also provide immediate feedback, reinforcing learning and allowing for personalized learning paths.

Next, we move on to
content delivery
. The manner in which information is presented is just as important as the information itself. Microlearning, the delivery of small, focused learning units, is highly effective for cybersecurity awareness. Instead of overwhelming employees with lengthy modules, break down the content into digestible chunks.
This approach caters to busy schedules and improves knowledge retention. Consider using a variety of media formats. Videos are excellent for explaining complex concepts, while infographics are ideal for presenting data concisely. Interactive simulations, such as phishing exercises, provide hands-on experience and reinforce learning in a practical setting. Think carefully about your target audience. Tailor the language and tone to their level of technical expertise. Using jargon unnecessarily can alienate and confuse learners. Incorporate real-world examples and case studies to demonstrate the relevance of cybersecurity principles. This helps learners connect the training to their everyday work experiences. Use relatable scenarios and characters to engage learners on an emotional level. For instance, instead of abstractly discussing the risks of phishing, you could illustrate the potential consequences with a realistic scenario of an employee falling victim to a phishing attack and the subsequent data breach. Explain the"why" behind the security policies, not just the "what."Understanding the rationale behind the rules is crucial for fostering compliance.

Assessment
is a crucial component of any effective e-learning module. It's not just about testing knowledge; it's about identifying knowledge gaps and reinforcing learning. Regular quizzes throughout the module help learners track their progress and identify areas where they need further review. Include a final assessment to evaluate overall comprehension. The assessment methods should align with the learning objectives, ensuring that the evaluation

accurately reflects the knowledge and skills acquired. Provide clear and constructive feedback after each assessment. This feedback should not only indicate correct or incorrect answers but also explain the rationale behind the answers. Furthermore, consider incorporating gamification elements into assessments. Leaderboards, badges, and points can incentivize learning and create a sense of accomplishment. Remember that the assessment is not simply a test but also a learning opportunity.

Accessibility
is a critical consideration. Ensure your e-learning module complies with accessibility standards (like WCAG guidelines) to make it usable by all employees, regardless of their abilities. This includes providing alternative text for images, using appropriate color contrasts, and offering transcripts for videos. Furthermore, consider offering different formats, such as text-based versions for learners who prefer this method. Remember to also provide options for learners with different learning styles; some people learn visually, while others prefer auditory or kinesthetic learning. Offering multiple modes of content delivery helps reach a broader audience and ensures that everyone can benefit from the training.

Finally, the choice of
learning platform
plays a significant role. There are many Learning Management Systems (LMS) available, each with its own set of features and capabilities. Choose a platform that aligns with your organization's needs and budget. The platform should integrate well with your existing IT infrastructure and be easy to use for both administrators and learners. Consider factors such as ease of content creation, scalability, reporting capabilities, and user support when selecting a platform. Some platforms offer built-in analytics and tracking tools that allow you to monitor learner progress and identify areas for improvement.

This data can be invaluable in refining your e-learning modules and enhancing their effectiveness.

Creating effective e-learning modules is an iterative process. Regularly review and update your modules to reflect changes in threats and best practices. Gather feedback from employees to identify areas for improvement. By incorporating this feedback and tracking the effectiveness of the modules using metrics such as completion rates, quiz scores, and post-training phishing simulation results, you can continuously refine your approach and maximize the impact of your cybersecurity awareness program. Remember, a successful cybersecurity awareness training program is a continuous cycle of improvement, feedback, and adaptation. It's an investment in your organization's future security, and effective e-learning modules are a crucial part of that investment. By carefully considering the design, content delivery, assessment, accessibility, and platform, you can create modules that empower employees to become active participants in protecting your organization. And don't forget the human element; ensure the modules are not merely informative, but also engaging, motivating and relevant to their daily work experience. This leads to better understanding, retention, and ultimately, a more secure workplace.

Incorporating Gamification and Interactive Exercises

Incorporating game mechanics into cybersecurity awareness training isn't just about adding fun; it's a powerful strategy to significantly boost engagement and knowledge retention. Traditional training methods often struggle to capture and maintain employee attention, leading to poor comprehension and ultimately, ineffective security practices. Gamification addresses this challenge by transforming learning into an enjoyable, competitive, and rewarding experience. By tapping into our natural desire for achievement, recognition, and social interaction, gamified training motivates employees to actively participate and learn, fostering a more proactive security culture within the organization.

One of the most fundamental aspects of gamification is the implementation of a points system. This simple yet effective mechanism rewards employees for completing training modules, answering quiz questions correctly, and successfully navigating simulated phishing attacks. Points accumulate, providing a tangible measure of progress and achievement. The accumulation of points can be visualized using progress bars, badges, or other visual cues, giving employees a clear sense of accomplishment as they move towards a defined goal. This continuous positive reinforcement encourages consistent participation and motivates employees to strive for higher scores. For example, an employee might earn 10 points for completing a module on password security, 5 points for correctly identifying a phishing email in a simulation, and 20 points for successfully completing a complex cybersecurity challenge. The points system can be tiered, offering different rewards or recognition for reaching specific milestones.

Leaderboards, another key element of gamification, inject a healthy dose of competition into the training process. By publicly displaying the top performers, leaderboards create a sense of friendly rivalry and encourage employees to push themselves to improve their scores. This competitive element is particularly effective in larger organizations where employees may not interact regularly with their colleagues. However, it's crucial to design the leaderboard system carefully to avoid creating a negative or exclusionary environment. For instance, instead of focusing solely on individual rankings, the leaderboard could also highlight team scores, encouraging collaboration and knowledge sharing. Furthermore, the leaderboard could be segmented based on departments or roles, providing a more relevant and engaging competition within specific teams. Regular updates to the leaderboard keep the competition fresh and maintain employee engagement over time.

Challenges, presented as puzzles, scenarios, or interactive simulations, provide a dynamic and engaging way to test employee knowledge and reinforce learning. These challenges should be carefully designed to reflect realistic cybersecurity threats and scenarios, enabling employees to apply their knowledge in practical contexts. For example, a challenge could involve navigating a simulated phishing campaign, identifying malicious links and attachments, and reporting suspicious activity. Successful completion of these challenges earns points and recognition, reinforcing the importance of vigilance and proactive security measures. The complexity of challenges can be gradually increased as employees progress, ensuring that the training remains challenging and engaging over time. A diverse range of challenges, incorporating various aspects of cybersecurity, keeps the training fresh and avoids repetitive exercises.

Beyond points, leaderboards, and challenges, there's a plethora of other gamification techniques that can be incorporated into cybersecurity awareness training. Badges, for instance, can be awarded for completing specific modules or achieving specific milestones. These badges can be visually appealing and serve as a testament to the employee's commitment to cybersecurity best practices. Similarly, levels or ranks can be introduced to signify increasing levels of expertise and knowledge. This structured progression system provides employees with a clear sense of advancement and a tangible reward for their efforts.

Another powerful gamification technique is the use of storytelling. Weaving cybersecurity concepts into narratives makes the learning process more engaging and memorable. Stories can be used to illustrate real-world security breaches, highlighting the consequences of poor security practices and the importance of vigilance. Alternatively, they can focus on successful security incidents, showcasing the positive outcomes of implementing appropriate security measures. The use of compelling storylines can make complex information easier to understand and retain.

To maximize the impact of gamification, it's vital to consider the target audience and their preferences. Different age groups and demographic groups may respond better to certain types of games or challenges. Therefore, it's advisable to conduct thorough needs assessments to understand the learning styles and preferences of employees, ensuring that the chosen gamification techniques are relevant and engaging to them. Regular feedback mechanisms, such as surveys or focus groups, provide valuable insights into the effectiveness of gamification and help to refine the training program over time.

Interactive exercises are crucial for translating theoretical knowledge into practical skills. These exercises should go beyond simple multiple-choice quizzes and delve into scenarios that mimic real-world situations. For instance, employees might be presented with a simulated phishing email and asked to identify the warning signs and report it appropriately. This hands-on approach allows them to apply their knowledge in a safe environment, reinforcing learning and building confidence. Interactive simulations can also involve navigating complex networks, identifying security vulnerabilities, or responding to security incidents. The interactive nature of these exercises keeps employees actively engaged and promotes deeper understanding.

The integration of gamification and interactive exercises requires careful planning and implementation. The chosen platform should be user-friendly, accessible across various devices, and capable of supporting the chosen gamification features. A well-designed gamified platform enhances the learning experience, motivating employees to actively engage with the training material. Furthermore, the platform should be capable of tracking employee progress and providing detailed feedback on performance. This data is critical for measuring the effectiveness of the training program and identifying areas for improvement.

To further enhance engagement, consider incorporating social elements into the gamified platform. For instance, allow employees to share their achievements, collaborate on challenges, and provide feedback to each other. This fosters a sense of community and encourages knowledge sharing among colleagues. It transforms the learning experience into a collaborative effort, promoting a culture of shared responsibility for cybersecurity.

Finally, it is important to ensure that the gamified training program aligns with the overall cybersecurity awareness strategy of the organization. The objectives of the training should be clearly defined and the gamification techniques should be tailored to support the achievement of these objectives. This ensures that the training is not simply entertaining but also effective in achieving its primary goal of improving cybersecurity awareness and practices. Regular evaluation and refinement of the gamified training program using metrics such as completion rates, scores on quizzes and challenges, and employee feedback, allows for continuous improvement and ensures that the program remains relevant and engaging over time. The long-term success of a cybersecurity awareness program hinges on its ability to adapt and evolve, ensuring that it continues to meet the needs of the organization and its employees. Gamification, when thoughtfully designed and implemented, can be a pivotal tool in achieving this crucial goal. By transforming learning into an enjoyable and rewarding experience, it significantly enhances employee engagement and leads to improved knowledge retention, fostering a more secure and resilient organization.

Conducting Effective Classroom Training Sessions

Effective classroom training remains a cornerstone of a robust cybersecurity awareness program, despite the rise of online learning platforms. While digital modules offer flexibility and scalability, the human interaction and immediate feedback possible in a classroom setting are invaluable for fostering genuine understanding and behavior change. The key to successful classroom training lies in moving beyond passive lecture formats and embracing interactive techniques that actively engage participants. This requires careful planning and a deep understanding of adult learning principles.

Before even stepping into the classroom, the facilitator should meticulously plan the session's structure and content. This involves aligning the training objectives with the overall cybersecurity strategy of the organization. What specific behaviors are you trying to modify? Are you aiming to reduce phishing susceptibility, improve password hygiene, or enhance the understanding of social engineering tactics? These objectives should be clearly defined and measurable, forming the foundation of the training's design.

A well-structured curriculum usually follows a logical progression, starting with a general overview of cybersecurity threats and their impact on the organization. This provides context and emphasizes the relevance of the training. Subsequent modules should delve into specific threats and vulnerabilities, offering practical advice and real-world examples. For instance, a module on phishing could include analyzing real-life phishing emails, discussing common tactics used by attackers, and demonstrating how to identify and report suspicious messages. This hands-on approach is far more effective than simply presenting theoretical information.

Instead of lengthy lectures, incorporate short, focused presentations interspersed with interactive activities. Consider using a variety of teaching methods to cater to different learning styles. Visual aids such as infographics, videos, and interactive simulations can enhance comprehension and retention. For example, a short video demonstrating a successful phishing attack followed by a group discussion on how the attack could have been avoided, is far more memorable than a lengthy lecture on the same topic.

Interactive exercises are crucial for maintaining engagement and ensuring active participation. Think beyond simple quizzes. Role-playing scenarios, where participants act out real-life situations involving cybersecurity threats, provide valuable practical experience and promote critical thinking. For instance, one scenario could involve a participant receiving a suspicious email and having to decide whether to click the link or report it. Another could involve a social engineering scenario where participants are required to identify and handle an attempt to gain access to sensitive information. The discussion that follows each scenario is equally important for highlighting the correct approach and reinforcing the key concepts.

Group discussions and brainstorming sessions allow participants to share their experiences and learn from one another. Encourage active participation by posing open-ended questions that prompt reflection and critical thinking. For example, "What are some common mistakes you've observed colleagues making regarding password security?" or "How can we improve our organization's response to phishing attacks?" These discussions help create a sense of community and foster a collaborative approach to cybersecurity.

Case studies provide powerful examples that illustrate the real-world consequences of poor security practices. Present a case study of a data breach or security incident, analyzing the contributing factors and the impact on the organization. This can drive home the importance of cybersecurity awareness and reinforce the need for responsible online behavior. A critical step after presenting the case study is conducting a discussion on what could have been done differently to mitigate the incident. This promotes learning from others' mistakes.

Hands-on activities, such as practicing password creation techniques using password managers, configuring multi-factor authentication (MFA), or using security scanning tools, help participants develop practical skills and build confidence. These activities provide opportunities for immediate feedback and reinforcement of concepts.

Incorporating quizzes and assessments is essential for evaluating learning outcomes. However, instead of focusing solely on scores, use them as a diagnostic tool to identify areas where participants need additional support. Follow-up sessions or supplemental materials can address these identified gaps. Also, provide feedback tailored to individual performance, not just a simple pass/fail grade. This personalized feedback increases the effectiveness of the training.

Throughout the training, maintain a positive and supportive learning environment. Create a safe space where participants feel comfortable asking questions and sharing their concerns. Avoid judgmental language and foster open communication. Remember that the goal is to promote learning and behavior change, not to instill fear or shame. By creating a supportive atmosphere, you will increase participation and knowledge retention.

After the classroom session, it's crucial to reinforce the learning experience through follow-up activities. This could involve providing additional resources, scheduling refresher sessions, or distributing reminders about key security practices. Furthermore, consider incorporating the Kirkpatrick Four Levels of Evaluation to measure the impact of your training. This involves measuring reaction (how participants felt about the training), learning (what participants learned), behavior (how participants changed their behavior), and results (the impact of the training on the organization's security posture). Collecting data on these levels allows for a comprehensive evaluation of the effectiveness of the training and identification of areas for improvement.

The effective use of technology in the classroom can significantly enhance the training experience. Interactive whiteboards, presentation software with integrated quizzes, and online collaboration tools can create a more engaging and dynamic learning environment. However, remember that technology should enhance the training, not replace the human interaction that is vital for effective learning and knowledge retention. It's a balancing act between leveraging technology's benefits while still prioritizing interactive elements and human connection.

Finally, consider the learning styles of your audience. Different individuals learn in different ways – some are visual learners, some auditory, and some kinesthetic. A successful training program should cater to all these styles by incorporating various teaching methods such as visual aids, discussions, and hands-on activities. This inclusive approach maximizes the effectiveness of your training and ensures that everyone benefits. Post-training surveys that assess participant satisfaction and identify areas for improvement are key to ensuring future sessions are even more effective. Regularly reviewing and updating your training materials based on feedback ensures relevance and continued effectiveness. Continual improvement is the cornerstone of any successful cybersecurity awareness program. By consistently evaluating and refining your classroom training sessions, you can create a program that is not only engaging but also profoundly impactful in shaping a more secure organizational culture.

Leveraging Microlearning for Continuous Improvement

Microlearning, with its bite-sized modules, offers a powerful approach to fostering continuous improvement in cybersecurity awareness. Unlike lengthy, monolithic training sessions that can overwhelm learners and lead to information overload, microlearning delivers content in easily digestible chunks. This approach caters to the increasingly short attention spans and busy schedules of modern employees. By focusing on specific cybersecurity concepts or threats, microlearning allows for a deeper understanding and better retention than traditional methods. For example, instead of a lengthy presentation on phishing attacks, a series of short videos could be used: one explaining what phishing is, another illustrating common phishing techniques, and a third outlining how to identify and avoid them. This modularity allows for targeted reinforcement of key concepts, improving knowledge retention significantly.

The effectiveness of microlearning is further enhanced by its adaptability. These short modules can be easily incorporated into existing workflows, making them less disruptive to employees' daily tasks. They can be accessed on demand, at any time and on any device, promoting a flexible learning environment. Imagine an employee taking a five-minute module on password security during a coffee break or reviewing a quick video on safe browsing practices during their lunch hour. This accessibility removes barriers to learning and ensures that critical information is readily available when employees need it. The convenience of microlearning is key to its success; it doesn't demand significant time commitments, enhancing engagement and compliance.

Furthermore, microlearning allows for personalized learning paths. Based on an employee's performance in assessments or their demonstrated risk behavior (e.g., clicking on suspicious links), the system can intelligently recommend specific microlearning modules to address their weaknesses. This personalized approach ensures that training is targeted and relevant to individual needs. Consider a scenario where an employee repeatedly fails a phishing simulation. A microlearning platform could automatically assign them targeted modules focusing on phishing recognition techniques, providing immediate and tailored feedback to address this specific weakness. This dynamic approach is far more effective than a one-size-fits-all training program, promoting continuous growth and improvement in cybersecurity awareness.

The implementation of microlearning should be strategic and integrated into the broader cybersecurity awareness program. It shouldn't exist in isolation but rather function as a supplementary tool alongside other training methods, such as classroom sessions or longer e-learning modules. Microlearning modules can be used to reinforce key concepts covered in other training formats, to address specific vulnerabilities identified through assessments, or as a refresher for employees who need to update their knowledge on specific topics. The key is to create a cohesive and interconnected learning experience. For example, a classroom session on data security could be followed by a series of microlearning modules focusing on specific data security policies within the organization, providing a deeper and more practical understanding.

Measuring the effectiveness of microlearning is crucial for optimizing its impact. Metrics like completion rates, assessment scores, and changes in employee behavior can provide valuable insights into the success of the program. Tracking completion rates helps identify any barriers to access or engagement, while assessment scores offer a clear indication of knowledge acquisition. Perhaps most importantly, measuring behavioral changes—such as a reduction in phishing susceptibility or improved password hygiene—demonstrates the real-world impact of the microlearning program. These metrics should be regularly reviewed and analyzed to inform adjustments to the content and delivery methods of the microlearning modules. For example, if completion rates are low for a particular module, it might indicate that the module is too long, too complex, or not relevant to the employees' needs. Adjustments can then be made to address these issues and improve the overall effectiveness of the program.

The development of effective microlearning modules requires careful planning and design. These modules need to be concise, engaging, and easy to understand. Visual aids, interactive elements, and gamification techniques can all be employed to enhance learner engagement and knowledge retention. Keep in mind the limitations of attention spans; avoid overwhelming learners with excessive text or complex concepts. Instead, focus on delivering information in short, focused bursts, using various methods such as videos, short quizzes, interactive scenarios, and infographics. Imagine a short video depicting a realistic phishing email, followed by an interactive quiz that tests the user's ability to identify the phishing indicators. Such a concise and engaging module will be much more effective than a lengthy PowerPoint presentation on the same topic.

The use of storytelling can dramatically increase engagement and memorability. Instead of presenting facts and figures in a dry manner, weave them into a narrative that captures the attention of the learners. Consider a scenario where a microlearning module uses a fictional case study to illustrate the consequences of a data breach, making the risks more tangible and relatable. Such an approach would resonate with learners more deeply than a simple list of security policies. The narrative should be concise and impactful, leaving a lasting impression on the learner's mind. A compelling story can create a lasting impact, encouraging learners to apply their knowledge in real-world situations.

Moreover, the creation of microlearning modules should involve a collaborative effort between cybersecurity professionals and instructional designers. Cybersecurity professionals provide the technical expertise and knowledge, while instructional designers bring their expertise in creating engaging and effective learning experiences. This interdisciplinary approach ensures that the modules are both accurate and effective in conveying the necessary information. Regular feedback from learners is also critical for ongoing improvement, enabling updates and adjustments to ensure that the modules remain relevant and effective. Continuous improvement is vital for maintaining the effectiveness of a microlearning program, so gathering and acting on feedback should be a top priority.

Gamification plays a significant role in boosting engagement and motivation within microlearning. Incorporating game mechanics, such as points, badges, leaderboards, and challenges, can transform learning into a fun and rewarding experience. This approach encourages learners to actively participate and strive for improvement. Imagine a microlearning module on password security that awards points for correctly answering security questions and badges for consistently using strong passwords. Such a gamified approach transforms a potentially dry topic into an engaging and rewarding learning experience, boosting learner engagement and knowledge retention. The use of leaderboards, while potentially controversial due to competitiveness, can create a friendly competition among colleagues, which often translates to improved knowledge retention across the group. However, careful consideration should be given to potential negative impacts and alternative approaches, like collaborative learning, should be incorporated to avoid overly competitive environments.

Finally, the success of a microlearning program depends heavily on its integration into the broader organizational culture. It should not be a stand-alone initiative but rather a component of a comprehensive cybersecurity awareness program. This integration involves incorporating microlearning into existing workflows, promoting its use through internal communication channels, and integrating it with other training methods. By embedding microlearning into the daily lives of employees, it becomes a normal part of their work, thereby increasing the likelihood of compliance and effective knowledge retention. Regular communication highlighting the importance of cybersecurity awareness and the role of microlearning in achieving this should be consistently reinforced through company newsletters, email announcements, and internal social media platforms. This concerted effort ensures that the microlearning initiative is not seen as an isolated training program but as a crucial element in fostering a security-conscious organizational culture. The long-term success of the program hinges on its consistent integration into daily operations and its alignment with the organization's broader security strategy.

Utilizing Email Marketing for Cybersecurity Awareness

Email marketing offers a powerful and cost-effective channel for disseminating cybersecurity awareness training and promoting a culture of security within an organization. Its reach extends to every employee, regardless of their physical location or role, making it a cornerstone of a multi-channel awareness campaign. However, the effectiveness of email-based cybersecurity awareness hinges on a strategic approach, encompassing compelling subject lines, engaging content, and clearly defined calls to action.

Crafting effective subject lines is paramount. A poorly conceived subject line often leads to emails being overlooked or deleted before they're even opened. Avoid generic subjects like "Security Update" or "Important Information," which are easily dismissed as spam. Instead, opt for personalized and intriguing subjects that pique the recipient's interest and highlight the value proposition of the email. For instance, "Protect Yourself from the Latest Phishing Scam," "Three Simple Steps to Improve Your Online Security," or "Learn How to Spot a Fake Website" are far more likely to capture attention. A/B testing different subject lines allows for data-driven optimization, identifying the most successful approaches for your specific audience.

The content of the email is equally crucial. Avoid lengthy, technical explanations that might overwhelm or bore the reader. Instead, focus on delivering concise, impactful messages that convey critical information clearly and concisely. Use bullet points, short paragraphs, and visuals like infographics or short videos to enhance engagement and understanding. Remember that attention spans are short, so prioritize clarity and brevity. For example, an email focusing on password security could highlight the importance of strong, unique passwords and offer practical advice on password management tools. It could also include a link to a short, interactive tutorial on creating secure passwords.

Another critical component of effective email marketing is the call to action (CTA). Every email should have a clear and compelling CTA, guiding the recipient toward the next step in the awareness process. This could involve clicking a link to a training module, taking a short quiz to test their knowledge, or reporting a suspicious email. The CTA should be strategically placed, using prominent visuals and clear language to encourage engagement. For instance, a button clearly stating "Take the Quiz Now!" or "Learn More About Phishing" is far more effective than a subtly placed link.

Beyond individual emails, consider creating a series of emails that build on each other over time. This approach fosters sustained engagement and encourages continuous learning. For example, you could begin with an introductory email outlining the importance of cybersecurity awareness and then follow up with emails focusing on specific threats, such as phishing, malware, and social engineering. Each email could build upon the previous one, gradually expanding the employee's knowledge base. This approach also allows for a measured rollout of information, preventing recipients from feeling overwhelmed with too much information at once.

Segmenting your email list based on job roles or department can also greatly enhance the effectiveness of your campaigns. Tailoring the content of emails to the specific needs and concerns of different employee groups ensures that the information is relevant and impactful. For instance, IT personnel might benefit from more technical information on security protocols, while administrative staff might require guidance on recognizing and avoiding phishing scams. A segmented approach maximizes engagement and ensures that the training resonates with its intended audience.

Regularity and consistency are key. Sending emails sporadically will not create a sustained level of awareness. Aim for a consistent schedule, perhaps a monthly newsletter highlighting current threats and best practices or weekly shorter emails focused on single, actionable tips. Consistency reinforces the message and keeps cybersecurity awareness at the forefront of employees' minds. A well-defined content calendar ensures a structured and planned approach to email dissemination.

Finally, don't underestimate the power of personalization. Addressing employees by name and tailoring the content to their specific roles demonstrates that the organization values their contribution to cybersecurity. This personalized approach fosters a sense of trust and credibility, making employees more likely to engage with the email and take action. Utilize data analytics to track the engagement rates and click-through rates of your emails. This allows you to fine-tune your strategy, optimizing the content, timing, and calls to action for maximum impact.

Beyond the content and structure of the emails themselves, the platform you choose for email distribution is equally important. Ensure your email service provider (ESP) complies with relevant data privacy regulations and can handle the volume of emails you intend to send. Robust ESPs often offer features like automation, A/B testing, and analytics dashboards that can significantly improve your campaign effectiveness. Regularly review your ESP's features and security protocols to ensure they remain current and aligned with your organizational security policies.

Furthermore, always include a clear unsubscribe option in your emails, respecting employees' rights to manage their communication preferences. While you aim for high engagement, forcing unwanted communications can have the opposite effect, potentially leading to resentment and a diminished willingness to participate in future initiatives. A professional and respectful approach throughout the email communication strengthens the trust between the organization and its employees, enhancing the overall impact of your cybersecurity awareness program.

Consider supplementing your email campaigns with other forms of communication. For instance, using email to announce a new training module or a phishing simulation can drive participation in these other awareness initiatives. This multi-channel approach ensures that your message reaches employees across multiple platforms, maximizing the likelihood of engagement and knowledge retention.

Integrating email marketing with other awareness tools, such as posters and intranet articles, creates a cohesive and comprehensive approach. For example, an email campaign might announce a new phishing simulation, directing employees to a dedicated intranet page with further instructions and resources. This integration creates a synergistic effect, reinforcing the message and driving greater participation in your broader awareness program.

Finally, always remember to measure the effectiveness of your email campaigns. Track open rates, click-through rates, and other key metrics to determine what is working and what is not. Use this data to continually improve your email strategy, ensuring that your messages are engaging, informative, and effective. By using a data-driven approach, you can optimize your email campaigns over time, leading to significant improvements in cybersecurity awareness within your organization. This iterative approach to email campaign management ensures that your efforts continue to evolve and adapt to the constantly changing landscape of cybersecurity threats.

Leveraging Posters Flyers and Digital Signage

Building upon the effectiveness of email campaigns, the next crucial element of a comprehensive cybersecurity awareness program involves leveraging the visual power of posters, flyers, and digital signage. These mediums offer a complementary approach, reinforcing key messages and reaching employees in physical spaces where email might be less effective or easily overlooked. The design and placement of these materials are critical to their success. A poorly designed poster, for example, can easily be ignored, while a well-placed digital sign can capture attention and deliver impactful information concisely.

The key to successful poster and flyer campaigns lies in strategic design and targeted placement. Avoid cluttered designs overloaded with text. Instead, focus on impactful visuals and concise, memorable messaging. Think strong imagery—a lock icon representing strong passwords, a shield symbolizing protection, or a stylized graphic representing data breaches. These visual cues immediately grab attention and communicate the core message without requiring lengthy reading. The text should be succinct, easily digestible, and focus on one key takeaway. For example, a poster promoting strong password creation could simply state: "Strong Passwords: Use at least 12 characters, including numbers, symbols, and uppercase letters." A flyer on phishing awareness might include a clear visual of a suspicious email and the advice: "Think Before You Click: Report Suspicious Emails Immediately!"

Consider the target audience when designing these materials. What kind of messaging will resonate most with them? Will a humorous approach be more effective, or a more serious and direct tone? Tailoring the messaging to your audience increases the likelihood of engagement and comprehension. For instance, a younger workforce might respond better to a more informal, perhaps even playful, design incorporating modern visuals and language, while a more senior workforce might appreciate a cleaner, more straightforward design with concise, easily understandable information. A/B testing different designs can help you determine what resonates best with specific employee demographics.

The choice of color is also critical. Use colors that are eye-catching but not overwhelming. Bright, contrasting colors can help your message stand out, but avoid using too many colors or a color scheme that is jarring or difficult to look at. The colors you choose should also be consistent with your company's branding to create a cohesive and professional look. Similarly, font selection is crucial. Choose a font that is legible from a distance, especially for posters and digital signage. Avoid overly stylized or decorative fonts that are difficult to read.

Placement is equally vital. Posters and flyers should be strategically placed in high-traffic areas where employees are likely to see them. This includes break rooms, hallways, near entrances and exits, and even in restrooms – locations where employees spend time and are more likely to engage with the content. Ensure posters are positioned at eye level for optimal visibility. Don't overcrowd the area with posters, as this can lead to message fatigue and diminished impact. Consider rotating posters regularly to maintain employee engagement and ensure the information remains fresh and relevant. Use a calendar system to schedule poster changes and ensure a consistent flow of information.

Digital signage provides another powerful avenue for disseminating cybersecurity awareness information. Unlike static posters and flyers, digital signage allows for dynamic content updates, enabling you to showcase timely alerts, reminders, and even short videos. This dynamic approach ensures the information remains current and prevents message fatigue. Integrate digital signage into your overall cybersecurity awareness program, using it to reinforce key messages delivered through other channels like email and training sessions. Use a consistent brand and messaging across all channels to build brand recognition and ensure clarity of the information presented.

For digital signage, consider using short, impactful video clips. These can effectively communicate complex information in an engaging and easily digestible format. Short animated videos, for instance, can visually illustrate phishing attempts or social engineering tactics, making the message more memorable than static text. Keep the videos concise – ideally, under 60 seconds – to maintain employee attention. You can also use digital signage to showcase statistics on data breaches, emphasizing the importance of cybersecurity practices.

Beyond static images and videos, incorporate interactive elements into your digital signage whenever possible. Interactive displays can engage employees more effectively than passive displays. This could involve quizzes, polls, or short games related to cybersecurity topics. This interactive approach enhances employee engagement and reinforces learning. Such interactive elements provide immediate feedback, allowing employees to test their knowledge and understand areas where they need further improvement.

Regularly update the content displayed on your digital signage. This prevents it from becoming stale and ensures that the information remains relevant and engaging. Use a content management system (CMS) to easily manage and update the content. Ensure that your digital signage content aligns with the overall cybersecurity awareness strategy and complements other awareness initiatives. Regularly assess the effectiveness of your digital signage and make adjustments based on employee engagement and feedback. Track metrics such as dwell time and engagement rates to measure effectiveness and inform future content strategy. Use data to refine your approach and improve the impact of your digital signage.

The effectiveness of posters, flyers, and digital signage, like any other component of your cybersecurity awareness campaign, needs to be measured. Although harder to directly quantify than email open rates, you can still track the impact. For posters and flyers, you might conduct periodic surveys to gauge employee awareness of the key messages displayed. Anecdotal feedback from employees can also be valuable. For digital signage, many platforms offer analytics showing dwell times and interaction rates. These metrics can help you assess the effectiveness of your approach and make informed decisions about content and placement.

Furthermore, integrate your visual campaigns with your other awareness efforts. If you're running a phishing simulation, for instance, use posters and digital signage to remind employees about the exercise and highlight key takeaways. This integrated approach reinforces messaging and maximizes the overall impact of your cybersecurity awareness program. Remember to consistently reinforce your core messages across all your channels. The repetition will help reinforce these important security concepts in the minds of your employees. This consistency is crucial for building a strong security culture within your organization. By strategically using posters, flyers, and digital signage alongside email and other methods, you create a multi-layered approach to cybersecurity awareness that maximizes reach and ensures a far greater chance of success. This holistic strategy is vital for creating a secure workplace where employees are informed, engaged, and actively contribute to the overall security posture of the company.

Employing Social Media and Internal Communication Channels

Building on the visual impact of posters and flyers, the next layer of our multi-channel approach involves strategically leveraging social media and internal communication channels. These platforms offer unique opportunities to reach employees in diverse ways, fostering engagement and reinforcing key security messages. However, unlike the more controlled environment of internal email or printed materials, social media requires a nuanced approach to ensure effective communication and avoid potential pitfalls.

Firstly, it's vital to understand your organization's internal social media landscape. Does your company utilize platforms like Microsoft Teams, Slack, Yammer, or internal blogs? These internal networks provide a controlled environment for sharing cybersecurity awareness content, bypassing the complexities and potential risks associated with external platforms. Internal communication channels are often already integrated into employees' daily workflows, making them ideal for delivering concise, relevant security updates and reminders.

Consider using these platforms to share short, engaging videos explaining security best practices. For instance, a brief video explaining the importance of strong passwords, using simple, relatable analogies, can be far more impactful than a lengthy written policy. Similarly, infographics illustrating phishing techniques or the consequences of data breaches can be shared easily and effectively. Remember to keep the content visually appealing and concise, catering to the attention spans of your audience. Break down complex topics into easily digestible chunks.

The use of interactive quizzes on internal platforms can significantly boost engagement. A short quiz testing employees' knowledge of common security threats, for example, can be both educational and fun. Furthermore, integrating leaderboards and friendly competition can encourage participation and reinforce learning. Consider offering small incentives, such as gift cards or recognition in company newsletters, to further motivate participation.

For companies with active external social media presences, extending the awareness campaign carefully can broaden its reach beyond the internal workforce. However, this requires a different strategic approach. While internal communication can be more direct and tailored to the specific needs of employees, external communication needs a more cautious and carefully considered strategy. Ensure any externally shared content is consistent with the company's brand guidelines and doesn't inadvertently reveal sensitive information.

When using external platforms like LinkedIn, Twitter, or even company blogs, focus on sharing valuable, industry-relevant information. Instead of directly addressing employees, aim for broader content that promotes cybersecurity awareness generally. Share articles on emerging threats, explain new security technologies, or highlight best practices for data protection. This approach builds the company's profile as a security-conscious organization, indirectly influencing employee behavior and reinforcing the importance of security.

Consider running social media campaigns around specific events, such as Cybersecurity Awareness Month. These campaigns offer structured opportunities to share relevant content and engage with followers. Use relevant hashtags to increase visibility and participate in industry conversations. However, be mindful of the tone and style of your messaging. Maintain a professional and informative tone, avoiding sensationalism or fear-mongering. Accuracy is paramount; always cite reputable sources for any statistics or information you share.

One particularly effective strategy on social media is to create a series of short, impactful videos or animated graphics that explain common security threats in a simple, engaging way. These could cover topics such as password hygiene, phishing scams, or the risks of public Wi-Fi. Consider utilizing humor where appropriate, but always ensure the message remains clear and informative. The visual nature of these formats caters to diverse learning styles and can significantly improve retention.

Internal communication channels also provide opportunities for personalized messaging. For example, you can tailor messages based on an employee's role or department. A security manager might need more in-depth information on a specific threat, while a receptionist might require a simpler, more focused message. This targeted approach ensures that the information provided is relevant and useful to the recipient, maximizing the impact of your communication.

Furthermore, actively encourage employee participation in the conversation. Ask questions, run polls, and respond to comments and feedback. This two-way communication builds trust and demonstrates your commitment to fostering a security-conscious culture. Involve employees in the development of security materials; their feedback can provide valuable insights and ensure that the messaging is relevant and relatable. Consider creating an employee feedback loop, allowing them to report suspicious activity or suggest improvements to existing security practices.

Remember that consistency is key. Regularly schedule posts and updates to ensure that cybersecurity awareness remains a consistent topic of conversation. Use a content calendar to plan your posts in advance, maintaining a steady stream of informative and engaging material. Don't overwhelm your audience with too much information at once; spread your content strategically to maximize its impact.

Consider using a combination of different content formats. Don't just rely on text-based posts. Incorporate videos, images, infographics, and interactive elements to keep the content fresh and engaging. Analyze the performance of your posts and adjust your strategy accordingly. Track metrics such as engagement rates, reach, and click-through rates to identify what works well and what needs improvement.

Finally, remember to always align your social media and internal communication strategy with your overall cybersecurity awareness program. Ensure that your messages are consistent across all channels and reinforce the key themes and messages of your broader initiative. By integrating social media and internal communication effectively, you can create a comprehensive, multi-faceted approach to cybersecurity awareness that fosters a culture of security within your organization. A collaborative and engaging approach, coupled with regular analysis and adjustments, will significantly enhance the effectiveness of your program and contribute to a stronger overall security posture. This holistic approach ensures that your security messages reach employees in diverse formats, maximizing engagement and knowledge retention. Furthermore, by demonstrating a commitment to continuous improvement, you'll foster a culture where security is not just a policy, but a shared responsibility.

Creating Engaging Videos and Animations

Building upon the engagement strategies discussed – leveraging social media, internal communications, and printed materials – we now delve into a powerful medium for cybersecurity awareness: video and animation. These dynamic formats offer unparalleled opportunities to capture attention, simplify complex concepts, and leave a lasting impression on employees. Unlike static posters or lengthy emails, videos and animations can transform abstract security risks into relatable scenarios, making cybersecurity training more engaging and effective.

The key to creating impactful videos and animations lies in understanding your audience and tailoring your content accordingly. A video explaining the dangers of phishing to a group of seasoned IT professionals will differ significantly from one designed for administrative staff less familiar with technical concepts. Consider the specific needs and technical proficiency of your target audience when planning your video's content and style.

For example, a video for IT professionals might delve into the technical details of a specific malware attack, showcasing its progression and the techniques used to mitigate it. This might involve screen recordings, technical diagrams, and expert commentary. On the other hand, a video targeting administrative staff could focus on real-world examples of phishing scams, highlighting the subtle cues that can identify a malicious email. This video might utilize compelling storytelling, actors portraying realistic scenarios, and clear, concise explanations. The choice of visuals, pacing, and language should always align with the audience's understanding and expectations.

Beyond audience segmentation, consider the platform where your video will be hosted. A short, snappy video ideal for social media platforms like Instagram or TikTok might be less suitable for a formal e-learning module. Similarly, a long-form video explaining complex concepts might be better suited for internal training platforms with pause and rewind options compared to a quick reminder on a company intranet. The length and style of your videos need to adapt to the viewing habits and expectations of each platform. Think about the attention spans of your audience members on different platforms.

High-quality production values are critical for credibility and engagement. Poorly lit, grainy videos with unprofessional narration can undermine the message and damage your organization's reputation. Invest in professional video production, or if budget constraints exist, use high-quality equipment and editing software, and consider utilizing the expertise of internal staff with video production skills. The use of professional voiceovers, engaging visuals, and compelling storytelling techniques can significantly enhance the effectiveness of your videos. Remember that a well-produced video is an investment in your employees' security and can significantly improve the overall effectiveness of your cybersecurity awareness campaign.

Animation offers unique advantages for explaining abstract concepts that can be difficult to portray in live-action footage. Imagine illustrating the process of malware propagation through a network using dynamic visuals. Animation allows you to visualize complex processes in a clear, concise, and engaging way. For example, you could visually represent data breaches, demonstrating the flow of sensitive information from an employee's computer to a malicious server. Similarly, visualizing the steps involved in a multi-factor authentication process can greatly improve employee understanding and adoption of this critical security measure.

Incorporating interactive elements can further enhance engagement with videos and animations. Interactive elements can range from quizzes and polls to branching storylines and simulations. These features transform passive consumption into an active learning experience, improving knowledge retention and application. For instance, a video on phishing awareness might include interactive elements that challenge viewers to identify legitimate emails from phishing attempts, fostering a more hands-on learning environment. Such interactive elements not only make the learning process more engaging but also offer an immediate assessment of the knowledge gained.

Furthermore, consider the use of microlearning techniques in your video production. Microlearning involves breaking down large chunks of information into small, digestible modules. This approach is particularly effective for delivering cybersecurity awareness training, as it allows employees to learn at their own pace and revisit specific concepts as needed. Rather than presenting a single long video, create a series of short videos focused on specific topics like password security, social engineering, or malware prevention.

Another crucial aspect is the integration of these videos into your wider cybersecurity awareness program. Don't treat them as standalone initiatives. Instead, ensure that your videos and animations reinforce the key messages and themes of your broader awareness campaign. For instance, a video could be part of a wider campaign focused on phishing awareness, supplementing emails, posters, and phishing simulations with a dynamic, engaging learning experience.

Consider cross-promotion across your various communication channels – a poster or email could promote the new video on phishing scams, directing employees to the company's learning management system or intranet.

Finally, the success of your video and animation initiatives should be measured and evaluated. Track metrics like video views, completion rates, and engagement with interactive elements. Incorporate feedback mechanisms, such as surveys or quizzes, to assess employee understanding and identify areas for improvement. This data is essential for demonstrating the effectiveness of your awareness program and making data-driven adjustments to your future video productions. Using Kirkpatrick's Four Levels of Evaluation, you can assess the effectiveness of your video at the reaction (how employees felt about it), learning (what they learned), behavior (if they changed their behavior), and results (if the program impacted the overall security posture) levels.

In conclusion, video and animation are powerful tools for enhancing cybersecurity awareness training. By carefully considering your audience, choosing the right platform, investing in high-quality production, integrating interactive elements, and employing effective measurement strategies, you can leverage these mediums to create truly engaging and impactful training materials. Remember that effective communication is key – tailor your approach to reach your target audiences, and focus on clarity, relevance, and engagement. The investment in creating compelling and informative videos will undoubtedly yield significant returns in a stronger, more secure organizational culture. By consistently employing these approaches, your cybersecurity awareness program will evolve into a dynamic and adaptive initiative, effectively fostering a culture of security within your organization. Remember that consistent improvement and adaptation are key to keeping the program relevant and engaging for your employees. The use of data-driven approaches to refine your video productions will lead to more successful and impactful training experiences. This, in turn, will ultimately translate into a more secure and resilient organization.

Developing Games and Interactive Simulations for Awareness

Building on the success of video and animation in cybersecurity awareness, we now explore the power of interactive games and simulations. These dynamic tools offer a unique opportunity to move beyond passive learning and actively engage employees in the process of understanding and mitigating cybersecurity risks. Unlike traditional training methods that often rely on lectures or rote memorization, games and simulations immerse learners in realistic scenarios, allowing them to experience the consequences of their actions (or inactions) in a safe and controlled environment. This hands-on approach fosters deeper understanding and better retention of crucial security concepts.

The design of effective cybersecurity games and simulations requires careful consideration of several key factors. Firstly, understanding your target audience is paramount. Are you designing for technical staff, executive leadership, or general employees? Each group possesses different levels of technical expertise and varying degrees of familiarity with cybersecurity concepts. Therefore, the complexity and content of the game must be tailored to the specific knowledge and skill level of your target audience. A game designed for experienced IT professionals will be vastly different from one intended for non-technical employees.

Secondly, the game's objective needs clear definition. What specific cybersecurity concepts are you hoping to teach? Are you aiming to improve password management skills, heighten awareness of phishing attempts, or enhance understanding of social engineering tactics? The game's design should directly address these learning objectives, providing clear and measurable outcomes. For example, a game designed to improve phishing awareness might present players with various emails, requiring them to identify and classify suspicious communications. Success in the game should be directly correlated with improved skills in identifying and avoiding phishing scams.

Furthermore, the choice of game mechanics should be carefully considered. Will it be a point-and-click adventure, a puzzle game, a strategy simulation, or something else entirely? The chosen mechanics should align with the learning objectives and the audience's preferences. Consider incorporating a variety of game mechanics to maintain engagement and prevent monotony. A blend of puzzles, challenges, and narrative elements can significantly enhance the learning experience.

Gamification techniques can further enhance the effectiveness of cybersecurity games and simulations. Incorporating points, badges, leaderboards, and rewards can motivate players and encourage participation. These elements create a sense of competition and accomplishment, making the learning process more enjoyable and rewarding. However, it's crucial to avoid making the rewards system the sole focus of the game. The primary goal remains effective cybersecurity education, and the gamified elements should serve to enhance, not distract from, the learning objectives.

When developing a cybersecurity game, consider the use of branching narratives. This allows for a personalized learning experience based on the player's choices and actions within the game. A branching narrative can present various scenarios and consequences, allowing players to explore different paths and learn from their mistakes in a safe environment. For instance, a game simulating a phishing attack could present players with several options in response to a suspicious email. Each choice could lead to a different outcome, highlighting the potential consequences of each action and reinforcing the importance of cautious behavior.

The level of realism in the game should also be carefully balanced. While aiming for realism is important, the game shouldn't be so difficult or frustrating as to discourage players. Striking a balance between challenge and engagement is crucial. If the game is too easy, it will fail to engage players and won't effectively reinforce the learning points. Conversely, if it's too difficult, it might lead to frustration and player dropout. Regular testing and feedback from the target audience are essential to fine-tune the game's difficulty and ensure an optimal learning experience.

Post-game analysis and feedback mechanisms are equally important. The game should provide players with feedback on their performance, highlighting areas where they excelled and areas needing improvement. This feedback can be delivered in the form of detailed reports or interactive summaries. It's also beneficial to incorporate a mechanism for players to self-assess their understanding of the covered concepts. This could involve quizzes or interactive exercises that test their knowledge and identify areas where additional training might be necessary.

Interactive simulations, a closely related approach, offer an alternative method for enhancing cybersecurity awareness. Unlike games, simulations often focus on mimicking real-world scenarios, such as a network attack or a data breach. The goal is to provide participants with a realistic experience of responding to a security incident, enabling them to develop practical skills in incident response and threat mitigation. For instance, a simulation might present players with a simulated phishing campaign, allowing them to analyze the attack vectors, identify compromised systems, and implement remediation measures. These simulations can be particularly effective in training security teams and incident response personnel.

The development of games and simulations often requires specialized skills and resources. Consider whether to build the game in-house or outsource the development to a specialized game development company. While building in-house offers greater control, it may require significant investment in time, resources, and expertise. Outsourcing can be a more cost-effective option, allowing you to leverage the expertise of experienced game developers. However, outsourcing necessitates careful selection of a vendor to ensure alignment with your learning objectives and brand standards.

Regardless of the chosen development path, thorough testing and iteration are critical. Pilot testing the game or simulation with a small group of employees before wider rollout can help identify and address any usability issues or bugs. Gathering feedback from the pilot group can provide valuable insights for improving the game's effectiveness and engagement. Iterative development, incorporating feedback and making necessary adjustments, is crucial for creating a high-quality learning experience.

Finally, the success of any cybersecurity awareness initiative, including games and simulations, must be measured. Employ Kirkpatrick's Four Levels of Evaluation – reaction, learning, behavior, and results – to assess the impact of the games and simulations on employee behavior and organizational security posture. Track metrics such as player engagement, completion rates, knowledge retention, and changes in employee behavior following the training. This data-driven approach allows for continuous improvement of the cybersecurity awareness program and demonstrates the ROI of the investment in game development. By systematically evaluating and refining your approach, you can ensure that your games and simulations consistently contribute to a stronger and more secure organizational culture. Remember that the goal is not just to create engaging games but to ultimately improve cybersecurity practices throughout the organization.

Understanding Kirkpatricks Four Levels of Evaluation

Kirkpatrick's Four Levels of Evaluation provide a robust framework for assessing the effectiveness of any training program, and cybersecurity awareness initiatives are no exception. Understanding and applying these levels is crucial for demonstrating the return on investment (ROI) of your program and justifying continued funding. This framework moves beyond simply measuring attendance or completion rates to delve into the actual impact on employee behavior and organizational security. Let's examine each level in detail:

Level 1: Reaction:
This is the most basic level of
evaluation, focusing on the participants' immediate reactions to the training. Did they enjoy the program? Did they find it engaging and relevant? This level is typically measured through post-training surveys or feedback forms. While seemingly simple, gathering this data is essential. Positive reactions often correlate with increased engagement and knowledge retention. However, it's important to note that a positive reaction alone doesn't guarantee behavioral change or improved security outcomes. Consider including questions about specific aspects of the training—was the material easy to understand? Were the activities helpful? Were the instructors engaging and knowledgeable? Open-ended questions allow participants to provide more detailed feedback. For example, a question like, "What was the most valuable aspect of this training?" can provide valuable insights into what resonated most with the audience. This type of qualitative data can inform future training design and content. Analyzing the reaction data might reveal areas for improvement, such as adjusting the pace of delivery,

simplifying complex concepts, or enhancing the interactive elements.

Level 2: Learning:

This level assesses the extent to which participants acquired knowledge and skills from the training.
This goes beyond simply measuring attendance; it focuses on actual knowledge gained. Effective methods for assessing learning include pre- and post-training assessments (quizzes or tests), knowledge checks embedded within e-learning modules, or even practical exercises that require applying learned knowledge. For instance, a pre-training quiz can gauge existing knowledge, while a post-training quiz evaluates the increase in knowledge after the training. The difference between the scores represents the learning gain. The questions should directly reflect the training's objectives, ensuring accurate measurement of knowledge acquisition. For example, if the training focused on phishing recognition, the assessment should include questions specifically testing the ability to identify phishing emails. The questions should be varied in format—multiple choice, true/false, short answer—to provide a comprehensive assessment. It's important to avoid overly technical language in your assessments to ensure they accurately reflect the knowledge gained by those with varying levels of technical expertise.

A critical aspect of Level 2 is ensuring the assessments are aligned with the training objectives. If the training aimed to improve password security practices, your assessment must specifically test whether participants understand and can apply best practices in this area. Analyzing the data from the learning assessments can pinpoint areas where the training was less effective or where additional reinforcement is needed. For example, if participants consistently struggle with certain concepts, it might indicate a need to revise the training materials or dedicate more time to those specific topics. Consider using different question types to gauge different levels of understanding. Multiple-choice questions can test recall, while short-answer or essay questions can evaluate comprehension and application of knowledge. By analyzing the strengths and weaknesses revealed in the learning assessment data, you can refine your training to ensure it effectively delivers the intended knowledge and skills.

Level 3: Behavior:
This is where the rubber meets the road.
Level 3 focuses on whether participants actually changed their behavior as a result of the training. This is arguably the most critical level, as it directly relates to the program's impact on security. It's difficult to directly observe behavioral changes across an entire workforce, so indirect measures are often used. These indirect measures might include observing improved security practices through monitoring systems, analyzing incident reports (a decrease in phishing clicks or reported security incidents post-training), or conducting follow-up surveys to inquire about changed behaviors.

For instance, you might track the number of phishing emails clicked before and after the training. A significant decrease in the click-through rate would suggest that the training effectively changed employee behavior. Similarly, a reduction in the number of reported security incidents could indicate improved awareness and responsible practices. You could also use simulations, such as realistic phishing exercises, to assess behavioral change. Analyzing employee responses to simulated phishing attacks can provide insight into the effectiveness of the training in fostering a more security-conscious behavior. Remember to debrief employees after simulations to reinforce lessons learned and provide further guidance.

Another method of assessing behavioral change is through observation and feedback from managers or supervisors. This provides valuable qualitative data. Supervisors might report observing employees applying newly learned skills, such as using strong passwords or reporting suspicious emails. By combining quantitative data (such as click-through rates) with qualitative feedback, a more holistic picture of behavioral changes emerges. The key to effectively measuring Level 3 is to choose appropriate metrics that directly relate to the training's objectives. For example, if the goal is to reduce the risk of social engineering attacks, then monitoring reports of social engineering attempts and successful attacks would be a crucial metric. These data points, combined with the feedback from supervisors and the behavioral insights from phishing simulations, help provide an accurate assessment.

Level 4: Results:
This is the ultimate measure of the training program's effectiveness. It focuses on the overall impact of the training on the organization's security posture. Did the training contribute to a reduction in security breaches? Did it improve the organization's overall security posture? Did it positively impact the bottom line by reducing the cost of security incidents? This level requires a broader perspective, often involving metrics such as a reduction in the number of successful phishing attacks, a decrease in the cost of data breaches, or an improvement in overall security scores from security assessments.

Level 4 evaluation is often more challenging than the previous levels because it requires connecting the training program's impact to broader organizational outcomes. This may involve analyzing data from various sources, including incident response logs, security audit reports, and financial records. For instance, a successful phishing simulation program might significantly reduce the number of employees falling victim to real-world phishing attacks, directly translating to a reduction in the risk of data breaches and associated financial losses.

Demonstrating the return on investment (ROI) for your cybersecurity awareness program is a crucial aspect of Level 4 evaluation. By quantifying the cost savings associated with fewer security incidents, you can build a compelling case for continued funding and investment in security awareness initiatives. This includes calculating the cost of security breaches avoided, the cost of remediation efforts saved, and the time saved by preventing security incidents. You can then compare these cost savings to the program's investment to determine the ROI.

In summary, Kirkpatrick's Four Levels of Evaluation provide a comprehensive framework for evaluating the effectiveness of cybersecurity awareness programs. By applying this framework and meticulously collecting and analyzing data at each level, you can gain valuable insights into your program's impact, demonstrate its ROI, and make data-driven adjustments to continuously improve its effectiveness, building a strong security-conscious culture within your organization. The process is iterative—the results from Level 4 evaluation often inform improvements needed at Levels 1, 2, and 3, leading to a continuous cycle of improvement. Remember that the value of this framework lies not just in the measurement itself but also in using the collected data to refine and optimize the awareness program, ensuring it remains relevant and effective in the ever-evolving landscape of cybersecurity threats. Using this structured approach transforms the training from a compliance exercise into a strategic initiative directly contributing to the organization's overall security and bottom line.

Collecting Data through Various Assessment Methods

Collecting data to accurately measure the effectiveness of your cybersecurity awareness program is crucial for demonstrating its value and identifying areas for improvement. This involves employing a variety of assessment methods, each offering unique insights into different aspects of the program's impact. A multi-faceted approach, leveraging several techniques, provides a more holistic understanding than relying on a single metric. Let's delve into some of the key data collection methods you can incorporate into your evaluation strategy, aligning them with Kirkpatrick's Four Levels of Evaluation.

Surveys: Gauging Knowledge, Attitudes, and Behaviors

Surveys are a versatile tool for gathering data at all four levels of Kirkpatrick's model. Pre-training surveys can establish a baseline understanding of employees' existing cybersecurity knowledge and behaviors. Post-training surveys can measure the increase in knowledge and assess changes in attitudes and intentions regarding security practices. These surveys should incorporate a mix of question types, including multiple-choice, rating scales (Likert scales), and open-ended questions.

For Level 1 (Reaction), surveys can assess learners' satisfaction with the training materials, delivery methods, and overall program experience. Questions might focus on the clarity of the content, the engagement level, and the relevance of the training to their roles. Positive feedback can help validate the effectiveness of the training approach, while negative feedback can pinpoint areas needing improvement.

Level 2 (Learning) assessment uses surveys to measure knowledge gained. This can be achieved through multiple-choice questions testing comprehension of key concepts, such as phishing recognition, password security, and social engineering tactics. These questions should directly relate to the training materials and should reflect the learning objectives outlined at the beginning of the training. Comparing pre- and post-training scores provides a clear indication of knowledge acquisition.

Level 3 (Behavior) evaluation relies on surveys to assess changes in employee behavior. Questions should directly address how employees intend to apply what they learned in their daily work. For example, you could ask, "How likely are you to report suspicious emails?" or "Do you now use stronger passwords than before the training?". These self-reported behaviors provide insights into the practical application of the training, although it's important to remember that self-reported data might not always reflect actual behavior.

Finally, Level 4 (Results) evaluation utilizes surveys to indirectly measure the impact of the program on organizational security. This might involve gauging the reduction in security incidents, phishing attempts reported, or the number of malware infections. While not a direct measure, the trend in these metrics can be correlated to the awareness training, providing an indicator of its broader impact. However, it's crucial to note that correlating these metrics to the training alone might not be enough; other factors could be at play.

Quizzes: A More Objective Measure of Learning

Quizzes, unlike surveys, offer a more objective measure of knowledge acquisition. They can be used to assess learning at Level 2 and provide a quantifiable measure of knowledge retention. Quizzes can be administered both pre- and post-training to gauge the impact of the program. A well-designed quiz should cover the key concepts covered in the training, using different question formats, including multiple-choice, true/false, and fill-in-the-blank, to comprehensively assess understanding. Ideally, the quiz should be sufficiently challenging to differentiate between those who mastered the material and those who did not. Anonymity can encourage honest responses.

The data collected from quizzes allows for a direct comparison of pre- and post-training scores, providing a numerical representation of knowledge gained. This quantifiable data is valuable for reporting on the effectiveness of the training program and demonstrating its impact. Analyzing the results can highlight areas where learners struggled and suggest improvements in the training content or delivery. Analyzing the specific questions missed can also reveal knowledge gaps and inform future training development.

Simulations: Assessing Real-World Application of Knowledge

Simulations, such as phishing simulations and simulated security incidents, provide a more realistic assessment of employees' ability to apply their cybersecurity knowledge in real-world scenarios. These are particularly effective for assessing Level 3 (Behavior) and, to a lesser extent, Level 4 (Results). Phishing simulations, for instance, involve sending realistic phishing emails to employees and measuring their response rate. Successful identification and reporting of these emails demonstrate practical application of the training.

The data collected from simulations offers a more objective measure of behavioral changes than self-reported data from surveys. The success rate in identifying and reporting phishing attempts provides a clear indication of how effective the training has been in changing employee behavior. This type of data is extremely valuable for demonstrating the program's impact on reducing organizational vulnerabilities. Analyzing the types of phishing attempts employees fell for can identify areas for improvement in future training.

Simulations beyond phishing can also be employed. These might include scenario-based exercises involving simulated security breaches where employees must make decisions based on their knowledge. These scenarios can simulate real-world threats, offering a more comprehensive evaluation of employees' ability to respond to security incidents. Analyzing the decisions made in these simulations allows for a more nuanced understanding of the training's impact on decision-making under pressure. Such exercises also help employees develop practical skills and build confidence in their ability to handle security incidents.

The analysis of simulation data should include not only the overall success rate but also an examination of the types of responses given. This can help identify areas where further training is needed and refine the approach to future simulations. For instance, are employees struggling with a particular type of phishing email or struggling to escalate security incidents effectively? Understanding these nuances allows for the creation of more targeted and effective training.

Incident Data: Measuring the Impact on Organizational Security (Level 4)

While not a direct measure of training effectiveness, data on security incidents, such as phishing attempts, malware infections, and data breaches, can indirectly indicate the program's impact on organizational security (Level 4). By tracking these metrics before and after the implementation of the awareness program, you can observe any trends that suggest a reduction in incidents. A decrease in reported phishing attempts, for example, could be attributed to improved employee vigilance as a result of the training. However, it is crucial to acknowledge that other factors may influence these metrics, making a direct causal link challenging to establish. Correlation does not equal causation. Therefore, a holistic approach, incorporating all assessment methods, is necessary for a robust evaluation.

The analysis of incident data requires a nuanced understanding of various contributing factors. A reduction in incidents might not solely be attributed to the awareness program; it could also be due to improved security infrastructure, updated policies, or external factors. To establish a strong correlation, a careful analysis is needed, considering these confounding variables. Ideally, this data should be compared with similar organizations that have not implemented such a comprehensive awareness program to help establish a benchmark. While not a direct measure of the training's success, it significantly contributes to demonstrating the overall positive impact of the program on the organization's security posture.

The key is to collect and analyze data from multiple sources to obtain a comprehensive picture. Combining survey data, quiz results, simulation outcomes, and incident data allows for a robust assessment of the program's effectiveness across all four levels of Kirkpatrick's model. This comprehensive data collection strategy enables a more accurate evaluation, informed decision-making, and allows for continuous improvement of the program to maximize its impact on organizational security. Furthermore, documenting this comprehensive approach provides valuable justification for continued investment in the cybersecurity awareness program. Remember, the ultimate goal is not just to deliver training but to foster a security-conscious culture within the organization, a goal that is most effectively achieved through continuous monitoring, evaluation, and refinement of the awareness program.

Analyzing Data and Reporting on Program Outcomes

Analyzing the data collected through the various methods outlined in the previous chapter is crucial for understanding the true impact of your cybersecurity awareness program. This analysis shouldn't be a simple tally of numbers; it requires careful interpretation to reveal meaningful insights and ultimately demonstrate the program's return on investment (ROI). This involves moving beyond simply reporting participation rates and delving into the behavioral changes observed, the reduction in security incidents, and the overall improvement in the organization's security posture.

The first step is to organize your data effectively. This may involve using spreadsheet software like Excel or dedicated data analysis tools. Consolidating data from different sources– surveys, quizzes, phishing simulation results, incident reports – into a centralized database is essential. Consistent labeling and clear categorization of data points will greatly simplify the analysis process. For example, instead of just recording the number of employees who completed a
training module, categorize responses based on department, role, or tenure to identify potential gaps in understanding or engagement across different groups within the organization. This granular level of data analysis allows for targeted improvements to the program.

Once your data is organized, the next step involves identifying key metrics and analyzing trends. For Kirkpatrick's Level 1 (Reaction), analyze the feedback received through surveys and post-training questionnaires. Look for patterns in the responses: were certain modules particularly engaging or confusing? Did participants find the training relevant to their roles? This qualitative data provides valuable insight into how to improve future training initiatives. Quantitatively, calculate average satisfaction scores and identify areas needing improvement based on specific feedback.

For Kirkpatrick's Level 2 (Learning), analyze the results of knowledge assessments (quizzes, tests) following training modules. Calculate average scores, identify knowledge gaps across different employee groups, and track the improvement in knowledge retention over time. This helps determine the effectiveness of the training content and identify areas where additional reinforcement is needed. For example, if scores on phishing awareness questions remain consistently low after multiple training attempts, it may indicate a need for a revised training approach or more frequent reinforcement activities.

Analyzing data from Kirkpatrick's Level 3 (Behavior) requires focusing on observed changes in employee behavior. This is where data from phishing simulations and incident reports becomes crucial. Compare the click-through rates on simulated phishing emails before and after training. A significant reduction in the click-through rate demonstrates a behavioral change, showcasing the program's success in teaching employees to identify and report suspicious emails. Similarly, analyze incident reports to identify a reduction in security incidents caused by human error, such as weak passwords or clicking on malicious links. A decrease in these incidents directly correlates to the effectiveness of the awareness program in altering employee behavior. This quantitative data is instrumental in demonstrating the program's ROI.

Kirkpatrick's Level 4 (Results) focuses on the overall impact of the program on the organization's security posture. This is the most challenging level to measure, often requiring a longer timeframe and potentially the integration of data from other security systems. Look for a reduction in security breaches, data loss incidents, or malware infections. While attributing these reductions solely to the awareness program can be difficult, a clear downward trend in security incidents following the implementation of the program strongly suggests its positive influence. This is where correlation, not necessarily causation, becomes a key aspect of your reporting. You can also track metrics such as the number of security incidents reported by employees, showcasing the program's success in fostering a culture of reporting. This can be further correlated with overall IT support ticket data to identify trends.

Beyond these core metrics, consider tracking additional data points, such as the cost per employee trained, the time spent on training, and the number of employees reached. This contextual information enhances the overall report and provides a more complete picture of program effectiveness. For example, a high participation rate might suggest a well-designed and engaging program, while a low participation rate might indicate the need for improved communication strategies or a better understanding of employee needs.

Once the data is analyzed, the next step is preparing a comprehensive report. This report should be concise, clear, and easily understandable by both technical and non-technical audiences. Begin with an executive summary that highlights the key findings and overall effectiveness of the program. Then, present the data using various visual aids such as charts, graphs, and tables to make the information more accessible and engaging. Include specific examples to illustrate the program's impact. For instance, if the phishing simulation click-through rate decreased by 60% after the program, highlight this achievement, demonstrating a significant return on the program's investment.

The report should clearly link the program's activities to the outcomes, illustrating how the investment in cybersecurity awareness translates into tangible benefits. Highlight areas of success and identify areas for improvement. Use the data to justify the continued investment in the program or to recommend adjustments to its strategy. If certain modules proved less effective, the report should recommend revisions or alternative training methods. Similarly, successful initiatives should be highlighted and scaled appropriately.

The final report should be presented to relevant stakeholders, including senior management, IT leadership, and other relevant departments. This presentation offers an opportunity to discuss the findings, answer questions, and obtain feedback. The insights gathered from this presentation can further inform future improvements to the program. Regularly reviewing and updating the program based on this feedback ensures that the program remains relevant, effective, and aligned with the ever-evolving threat landscape.

Remember that measuring program effectiveness is an ongoing process. Continuous monitoring and evaluation allow for continuous improvement and demonstrate the commitment to improving cybersecurity posture. The data collected not only measures the success of the program but also provides valuable insights for refining future initiatives, strengthening the organization's overall security posture, and justifying further investment in cybersecurity awareness training. The process of collecting, analyzing, and reporting on data isn't just about numbers; it's about building a culture of security, proving its value, and ultimately safeguarding the organization. This iterative process ensures the program adapts to evolving threats and maintains its effectiveness over time. By effectively measuring and reporting on the outcomes, you can secure buy-in from leadership, demonstrate a clear return on investment, and foster a culture of proactive cybersecurity within your organization.

Using Metrics to Demonstrate ROI and Justify Budget Requests

Demonstrating the value of a cybersecurity awareness program goes beyond simply showing participation rates. To secure continued funding and resources, you need to articulate the program's return on investment (ROI) in concrete, measurable terms. This requires a shift from qualitative assessments to quantitative data, leveraging key performance indicators (KPIs) to showcase the tangible benefits of your efforts. The KPIs you choose will depend on your organization's specific goals and priorities, but some key metrics consistently demonstrate ROI and bolster budget justification.

One powerful KPI is the **reduction in phishing susceptibility**. By tracking the number of employees who fall victim to phishing attempts before and after the implementation of your awareness program, you can quantify its effectiveness in improving user awareness and behavior. This data can be obtained through controlled phishing simulations, where employees are sent simulated phishing emails to test their vigilance. A significant decrease in the click-through rate and successful attacks directly demonstrates the program's impact on reducing a major security risk. For example, if your pre-program phishing success rate was 25% and post-program it dropped to 5%, this represents a striking 80% reduction – a compelling statistic to present to budget holders. Furthermore, you can detail the potential cost savings averted by preventing successful phishing attacks, calculating the potential losses from data breaches or malware infections. This concrete demonstration of cost avoidance is highly persuasive.

Another crucial KPI is the
decrease in security incidents
. This metric encompasses a broader range of security threats, including phishing, malware infections, accidental data leaks, and violations of security policies. By meticulously tracking the number and type of security incidents before and after program implementation, you can build a
compelling case for the program's effectiveness in enhancing overall security posture. For example, a 30% reduction in reported security incidents after implementing the program shows tangible results. However, simply reporting the decrease isn't enough. You need to correlate this decrease to the specific training modules or campaigns implemented, illustrating a clear cause-and-effect relationship. Presenting this data visually, using charts and graphs, will make the information more accessible and impactful for those reviewing your budget request.

Beyond incident reduction, you can measure the
improvement in security knowledge and awareness
. This can be assessed through pre- and post-training assessments, quizzes, or surveys. Tracking the improvement in employees' understanding of security policies, threats, and best practices provides valuable evidence of the program's impact on
knowledge acquisition. A substantial increase in average test scores after the program demonstrates the effectiveness of the training materials and delivery methods. For instance, a 20% increase in average test scores after a security awareness training program directly correlates with increased knowledge. This data strengthens your argument, showing that your investment in training translates into a better-informed and more security-conscious workforce.

Furthermore, consider measuring
employee engagement and participation
. High participation rates in training programs and activities reflect employee buy-in and indicate the program's relevance and effectiveness. Measuring

metrics like completion rates for online modules, attendance at workshops, and participation in phishing simulations provides insights into employee engagement. If your program boasts high participation rates coupled with reduced incidents and improved knowledge scores, it paints a holistic picture of success. For instance, showcasing a 90% completion rate for online training modules coupled with a reduction in security incidents provides irrefutable evidence of program success. This level of engagement not only bolsters your budget request but also demonstrates employee commitment to security, fostering a culture of security within the organization.

Beyond these core KPIs, consider incorporating more nuanced metrics relevant to your organization's specific security challenges. For instance, if you've experienced a rise in insider threats, you can measure the reduction in unauthorized access attempts after implementing a program focusing on data security and access control. Or, if your concern is around compliance, you can measure improvements in compliance scores after deploying training on relevant regulations. The key is to choose KPIs that directly address your organization's most pressing security risks and tailor your reports to highlight the positive impacts of your program in those areas.

To effectively present this data and justify your budget, remember that storytelling is crucial. Don't just present numbers; contextualize them within a narrative that clearly outlines the problem, the solution (your cybersecurity awareness program), and the positive outcomes. Use visual aids such as charts and graphs to present the data clearly and concisely, and quantify the cost savings achieved by preventing security incidents. For instance, you can translate a 15% reduction in phishing attacks into a dollar amount by estimating the cost of a data breach. This provides a powerful demonstration of ROI that is readily understandable by stakeholders.

When crafting your budget request, explicitly link the requested funds to specific program improvements or expansions. For example, if you're requesting funds to develop new e-learning modules, explain how these modules will address a specific knowledge gap identified through your KPI analysis. Or, if you're requesting funds for more frequent phishing simulations, explain how this will maintain employee vigilance against evolving threats. By clearly articulating the need and demonstrating a clear path to further improvements, you can increase the likelihood of securing the necessary resources.

The process of measuring program effectiveness is iterative. Regularly review and analyze your KPIs, and adjust your program's content and delivery methods based on the data. This ongoing evaluation demonstrates continuous improvement and a commitment to enhancing your organization's security posture. Regular reporting, not just at budget renewal time, but also throughout the year, showcases the program's ongoing effectiveness and keeps stakeholders informed of its value. This consistent communication builds trust and enhances your credibility. By proactively demonstrating the value of your program, you will not only secure future funding but also cultivate a more secure and resilient organization. Remember, your cybersecurity awareness program is an investment, not an expense. By effectively demonstrating its ROI, you can transform it into a strategic asset that protects your organization's valuable assets and reputation. The investment in continuous measurement and improvement will ultimately yield greater returns in the long run, strengthening your organization's overall security posture.

Improving Program Effectiveness Based on Data Analysis

Improving program effectiveness hinges on a robust data analysis process. Simply tracking participation rates is insufficient; a deeper dive into the data is crucial to understand what's working, what's not, and how to optimize your cybersecurity awareness program for maximum impact. This involves moving beyond simply gathering metrics to actively interpreting the data to identify trends, pinpoint weaknesses, and inform strategic adjustments. This iterative process ensures continuous improvement and maximizes the return on investment (ROI) of your program.

One crucial aspect of data analysis is identifying the specific areas where employees demonstrate vulnerabilities. For instance, if your phishing simulation reveals a high click-through rate on a particular type of lure—say, an email claiming a package delivery requires immediate action—this pinpoints a weakness in your training materials. The data highlights that your current education on recognizing and handling phishing attempts related to package deliveries is insufficient. This informs the need to revise training content to specifically address this vulnerability, focusing on educating employees on recognizing suspicious emails concerning deliveries, emphasizing verification steps, and highlighting common deceptive tactics used in such scams. This targeted approach, driven by data analysis, ensures that future training directly addresses the specific vulnerabilities identified.

Similarly, analyzing the results of knowledge assessments can reveal gaps in employee understanding of key cybersecurity concepts. If a significant portion of employees consistently fail questions related to password security, for example, it indicates a need to reinforce this area in future training modules. Instead of relying on generic presentations, you might incorporate interactive modules with scenarios and quizzes, or gamified challenges to improve engagement and knowledge retention. The data-driven approach ensures your program addresses the precise needs of your workforce, maximizing its impact and mitigating risk more effectively.

Beyond individual assessments, analyzing data across different demographic groups within your organization can reveal disparities in understanding or engagement. For example, you might find that certain departments consistently score lower on knowledge assessments or exhibit higher click-through rates in phishing simulations. This data suggests that these departments require more targeted or specialized training. Perhaps their roles expose them to different types of threats, necessitating tailored content and delivery methods. Perhaps their daily workflow prevents them from engaging with the training in the same way as other departments. Understanding these nuances allows you to develop differentiated training strategies to ensure that all employees, regardless of role or department, receive the appropriate level of security awareness education.

Data analysis isn't simply about identifying weaknesses; it's also about celebrating successes and reinforcing positive behaviors. If a particular training module consistently achieves high scores on knowledge assessments or significantly reduces click-through rates in phishing simulations, it indicates a successful approach that should be replicated or expanded upon. Understanding which elements of your program resonate most with your employees allows you to optimize your resources and focus on what yields the best results. Recognizing and rewarding success also boosts morale and demonstrates the value of the program to employees, reinforcing their commitment to cybersecurity best practices.

The use of A/B testing can further enhance your data analysis. By running two versions of a training module or phishing simulation with slightly different approaches—for instance, one using gamification and the other a more traditional lecture-style approach—you can collect data to determine which method is more effective. This allows you to refine your delivery methods based on empirical evidence, ensuring that your training is engaging and impactful. Analyzing the results of A/B tests not only improves the effectiveness of your individual training modules but also provides valuable insights into the learning styles and preferences of your employees.

The effectiveness of different communication channels can also be analyzed using data. Are employees more engaged with email communications, posters in the workplace, or online learning modules? Analyzing the engagement metrics for each channel—open rates for emails, click-through rates on links, completion rates for online modules, and so on— helps you optimize your communication strategy and focus your efforts on the channels that yield the best results. This data-driven approach ensures that your messages reach your employees in a format they are most likely to engage with, maximizing the impact of your cybersecurity awareness campaigns.

Furthermore, examining the temporal aspect of your data can reveal important patterns. Are there specific times of year when employees are more vulnerable to phishing attacks or demonstrate weaker knowledge of cybersecurity best practices? For example, you might find that phishing simulation click-through rates are higher during periods of increased workload or stress. This understanding allows you to adjust your training schedule and content to address these vulnerabilities proactively. By recognizing seasonal fluctuations in vulnerabilities, you can tailor your training programs to reinforce important security concepts during high-risk periods.

Analyzing the type of phishing attempts that successfully tricked employees allows you to understand which tactics are most effective for attackers. This knowledge is invaluable for refining your training to specifically address these techniques. For example, if many employees fall victim to spear-phishing attempts, focusing on training that addresses the sophistication and personalization of spear-phishing attacks is crucial. This data-driven approach allows you to not only improve your awareness training but also allows you to better understand and anticipate evolving attack methods.

To effectively analyze this data, you should utilize data visualization tools. Charts, graphs, and dashboards can make complex data easily understandable, highlighting trends and patterns in a clear and concise manner. This is especially useful when presenting the data to stakeholders who may not be cybersecurity experts. Using visual representations, you can effectively communicate the results of your data analysis, demonstrating the impact of your cybersecurity awareness program and justifying the need for continued investment. These visual aids make the data more accessible and convincing, fostering buy-in from stakeholders and supporting future budget allocation.

Finally, remember that data analysis is an ongoing process. Regularly review your KPIs and adjust your training methods accordingly. This iterative approach ensures that your cybersecurity awareness program remains relevant, effective, and aligned with the evolving threat landscape. Consistent monitoring and adjustment demonstrate a commitment to continuous improvement, strengthening the program's effectiveness and enhancing your organization's overall security posture. The continuous nature of this process is paramount; it showcases a proactive and adaptable approach to cybersecurity awareness, constantly enhancing its effectiveness and demonstrating ongoing value. The process of continuous improvement, driven by data analysis, is a key factor in maintaining a robust and effective cybersecurity awareness program.

Promoting a SecurityConscious Workplace Culture

Cultivating a security-conscious workplace culture isn't a one-time event; it's an ongoing process requiring consistent effort and strategic planning. It's about embedding security awareness not just into training programs, but into the very fabric of the organization's daily operations and values. This involves more than just delivering training modules; it requires a fundamental shift in mindset, where security becomes a shared responsibility, not just the domain of the IT department.

One of the first steps in promoting this culture is fostering open communication. Employees need to feel comfortable reporting security incidents without fear of reprisal. This requires creating a culture of trust and psychological safety, where mistakes are seen as learning opportunities rather than grounds for disciplinary action. Establish clear reporting channels – maybe a dedicated email address, a hotline, or a secure online portal – and ensure that all reports are handled promptly and confidentially. Regularly communicate to employees how their reports are being investigated and what actions are being taken as a result. This transparency builds confidence and encourages further reporting.

Consider implementing a "security champion" program, where employees from different departments are trained to act as internal advocates for security best practices. These champions can help disseminate information, answer questions, and act as a liaison between the IT department and the rest of the workforce. They can also help to tailor security messages to resonate with the specific concerns and needs of their respective departments. This peer-to-peer approach can be far more effective than top-down mandates. The champions should be well-trained, empowered, and recognized for their contributions.

Regular communication is crucial. This isn't just about sending out occasional security bulletins; it's about integrating security awareness into regular internal communications. Consider using internal newsletters, intranet articles, team meetings, and even company-wide announcements to keep security top-of-mind. Tailor your messages to different audiences, using language and examples relevant to their roles and responsibilities. For instance, a message about safe password practices might be different for a software developer than for a marketing assistant. The key is to make the information relevant, digestible, and easily understood by everyone.

Reinforce the importance of security through consistent messaging. Use a variety of mediums – posters, flyers, email campaigns, videos – to drive home key messages. Keep the messaging consistent, using similar terminology and branding across all channels. The repetition will help reinforce the importance of security and make it a part of the everyday conversation. Regularly review and update your communication materials to reflect the latest threats and best practices. Static messaging quickly becomes outdated and loses its impact.

Regular security awareness training sessions should be integrated into the company's overall training schedule. These sessions shouldn't be isolated events; they should be woven into onboarding programs, annual reviews, and even team-building activities. This ensures that security awareness is consistently reinforced, and employees are reminded of best practices on a regular basis. Consider using interactive games, quizzes, and simulations to make the training engaging and memorable. Avoid lengthy lectures and focus on delivering bite-sized information that is easy to understand and apply.

Another critical aspect is recognizing and rewarding employee contributions to security. This could involve offering public acknowledgment in company newsletters, providing gift cards or other small tokens of appreciation, or offering opportunities for career advancement. This demonstrates that the organization values its employees' commitment to security and encourages them to continue their contributions. Consider establishing a formal process for recognizing and rewarding security achievements, which could include an awards program or a system for nominating employees for special recognition.

Furthermore, security incidents should be viewed as opportunities for learning and improvement. When an incident occurs, conduct a thorough investigation to understand the root cause and to identify any gaps in the awareness program. Communicate the findings and lessons learned to all employees. This demonstrates transparency and accountability and also reinforces the message that the organization takes security seriously. Don't just focus on blame; focus on identifying weaknesses in the system and implementing improvements. Conduct post-incident training to reinforce relevant security practices and prevent future incidents.

Finally, establish a continuous improvement cycle for your cybersecurity awareness program. Regularly evaluate the effectiveness of your program using metrics like phishing simulation success rates, security incident reports, and employee feedback. Use this data to identify areas for improvement and make adjustments to your strategy. This ensures that the program remains relevant and effective in the face of constantly evolving threats. Consider establishing a regular review process – perhaps quarterly or annually – to assess the program's performance and plan for future enhancements. Regular updates ensure that the program stays current with the latest threats and best practices.

The creation of a security-conscious culture is an investment in the long-term security of the organization. It's not just about reducing the risk of cyberattacks; it's about creating a workplace where employees feel empowered to take responsibility for their own security and the security of the organization as a whole. By fostering open communication, implementing a variety of engagement strategies, rewarding positive behavior, and learning from mistakes, organizations can build a culture where security is everyone's concern and responsibility. This integrated approach ultimately leads to a stronger, more resilient security posture and a workplace where everyone feels secure. Remember, building a security-conscious culture isn't a destination; it's a journey requiring ongoing effort, adaptation, and a commitment to continuous improvement. The rewards, however, are immeasurable: a safer, more productive, and more secure work environment for everyone.

Encouraging Employee Feedback and Participation

Building a truly effective cybersecurity awareness program requires more than just delivering training; it demands active engagement and participation from employees at all levels. A top-down approach, where security awareness is dictated rather than cultivated, will inevitably fall short. To truly foster a culture of security, organizations must create channels for open communication, actively solicit employee feedback, and incorporate that feedback into the ongoing evolution of their awareness programs. This participatory approach is crucial for several reasons: it increases buy-in, identifies program weaknesses, and ensures the program remains relevant and engaging.

One of the most effective methods for encouraging feedback is to establish regular communication channels dedicated solely to cybersecurity awareness. This could take the form of a dedicated email address, a secure online feedback form, or even a suggestion box – physical or virtual – where employees can anonymously submit their thoughts, concerns, and suggestions. The key is to make the process as simple and accessible as possible. A cumbersome or overly complicated feedback mechanism will quickly discourage participation. For instance, requiring employees to navigate a complex internal portal to submit feedback is likely to result in low response rates. Instead, a simple, easily accessible online form with clear instructions and minimal fields will significantly increase participation.

Beyond the simple act of providing a platform for feedback, organizations must actively promote its use. Regular announcements – through email newsletters, internal communications platforms, or even company-wide meetings– should remind employees of the availability of these feedback channels and emphasize the importance of their input. These announcements should highlight the organization's commitment to continuous improvement and the role employee feedback plays in shaping the effectiveness of the cybersecurity awareness program. For example, a regular email could announce a new feedback campaign and outline specific areas the organization is looking for input on, such as the effectiveness of recent training modules or suggestions for improvement.

Furthermore, organizations should actively demonstrate that feedback is valued and acted upon. This requires a transparent process where feedback is reviewed, analyzed, and, most importantly, acted upon. Simply collecting feedback without demonstrating any tangible action is a recipe for disengagement. Regular updates, either via email or internal communication platforms, outlining how employee feedback has been used to improve the program, build trust and encourage future participation. For instance, if employees consistently report difficulty understanding certain training materials, the organization can use this feedback to revise the materials, simplifying the language or adding more visuals. If a particular phishing simulation proved ineffective, the organization can use this feedback to refine future simulations, making them more realistic and engaging.

Implementing anonymous feedback mechanisms is equally critical. Many employees may hesitate to voice their concerns openly, fearing retribution or judgment. Anonymous feedback allows for honest and unfiltered input, providing valuable insights that might otherwise remain hidden. This anonymity must be genuinely guaranteed; employees must be assured that their identities will remain completely confidential. Using third-party survey tools with robust privacy features can help to ensure this confidentiality. Transparency about how this anonymous feedback is analyzed and used – outlining the processes for data aggregation and anonymization – further reinforces trust and encourages participation.

Beyond formal feedback mechanisms, informal opportunities for engagement should be created. Regular informal meetings, workshops, or even casual discussions with security personnel can provide valuable opportunities for employees to express their concerns, ask questions, and share their experiences. These interactions create a sense of community and shared responsibility, making security a more relatable and less intimidating topic. This could involve organizing lunchtime brown bag sessions where employees can informally discuss cybersecurity issues, or hosting interactive Q&A sessions with cybersecurity experts. These informal channels often reveal insights missed through formal feedback mechanisms.

Another effective strategy is to incorporate gamification into the feedback process. For example, organizations could introduce a points-based system where employees receive points for submitting valuable feedback, participating in surveys, or attending security awareness workshops. These points could then be redeemed for rewards, such as gift cards, extra vacation time, or recognition in company newsletters. Gamification can significantly boost engagement and make the process more fun and rewarding. The rewards themselves should be carefully selected to reflect the organizational culture and employee preferences. For example, a younger workforce might be more motivated by gift cards or tech gadgets, while an older workforce might prefer extra vacation time or company recognition.

Furthermore, employee participation can be encouraged through active involvement in the design and development of security awareness programs. This participatory approach fosters a sense of ownership and commitment, ensuring the program aligns with the needs and experiences of the employees it is designed to protect. Involving employees in focus groups or surveys during the development phase allows them to shape the program from its inception, ensuring it resonates with their individual needs and preferences. This approach is particularly valuable when targeting diverse employee demographics or those with varying levels of technical expertise. By actively involving employees in the creation of the programs, organizations can ensure the message is not only understood but also resonates with the audience.

Regularly auditing and evaluating the effectiveness of the feedback mechanisms is essential. Are employees using the channels provided? Is the feedback received providing valuable insights? Is the feedback being incorporated effectively into program improvements? Regular analysis of feedback mechanisms can help identify areas for improvement and ensure the systems are functioning as intended. This evaluation should also incorporate quantitative and qualitative data analysis to obtain a holistic view of employee perceptions and program effectiveness. For example, analyzing survey responses alongside participation rates in training programs and phishing simulation results provides a comprehensive picture of the overall impact of the feedback mechanisms. The findings from this analysis can then be used to inform improvements to the feedback systems, making them more effective and encouraging increased participation.

Finally, successful feedback mechanisms are only possible in an environment of trust and open communication.

Employees must feel safe expressing their concerns without fear of repercussions. Organizations need to foster a culture where mistakes are seen as learning opportunities rather than grounds for punishment. This requires consistent reinforcement of the organization's commitment to a secure work environment and clear communication about the importance of employee participation in achieving this goal. Building a culture of trust and openness is crucial for maximizing employee engagement and ensuring that cybersecurity awareness programs are effective and relevant. Transparency and open dialogue are essential for creating a safe space where employees feel comfortable contributing their feedback.

In conclusion, actively soliciting and incorporating employee feedback into cybersecurity awareness programs is vital for cultivating a truly security-conscious culture. This requires establishing readily accessible feedback channels, actively promoting their use, demonstrating a clear commitment to acting on the feedback received, and fostering an environment of trust and open communication. By prioritizing employee engagement, organizations can significantly improve the effectiveness of their security awareness programs, leading to a more secure and resilient workplace. The continuous feedback loop, incorporating suggestions for improvements and actively showing the resulting changes, directly contributes to a more engaged and secure workforce. This proactive approach not only strengthens the organization's security posture but also empowers employees to take an active role in protecting sensitive information and maintaining a safe working environment for everyone.

Recognizing and Rewarding Employee Contributions to Security

Building a culture of security isn't solely about delivering training; it's about fostering a sense of shared responsibility and ownership. A crucial element in this process is recognizing and rewarding employees for their contributions to the organization's security posture. This isn't just about acknowledging exceptional feats; it's about reinforcing positive behaviors and encouraging proactive security practices across the entire workforce. A robust rewards program, thoughtfully designed and consistently implemented, can significantly bolster the effectiveness of any cybersecurity awareness initiative.

The most effective reward programs move beyond simple monetary incentives. While bonuses and gift cards certainly hold appeal, a truly comprehensive approach incorporates a variety of rewards tailored to individual preferences and motivations. Some employees may be deeply motivated by public recognition, while others may prefer more private acknowledgment. Understanding this diversity is key to designing a system that resonates with everyone.

One highly effective method is to implement a formal "Security Champion" program. This involves identifying employees who consistently demonstrate exceptional security awareness and proactively contribute to the organization's security efforts. These champions can be nominated by their peers, managers, or even identified through analysis of security logs (e.g., individuals who consistently report suspicious emails or activities). Recognizing these individuals formally, perhaps with a dedicated award ceremony or a feature in the company newsletter, can significantly boost morale and encourage others to emulate their behavior. The title of "Security Champion" itself carries weight, providing a sense of accomplishment and recognition for those who actively contribute to the organization's security.

Beyond formal recognition programs, informal acknowledgment also plays a vital role. A simple "thank you" from a manager or a peer can go a long way in reinforcing positive behaviors. Publicly praising an employee for securely handling sensitive data or for reporting a potential security threat during a team meeting can significantly impact the overall security culture. These small gestures, consistently practiced, collectively create a powerful reinforcing effect, encouraging proactivity and vigilance.

Furthermore, incorporating employee suggestions into the cybersecurity awareness program itself demonstrates a commitment to their input and strengthens their sense of ownership. If an employee suggests a particularly effective training module or a more engaging communication method, incorporating their idea and crediting them for it can create a significant positive impact. This not only strengthens the program but fosters a sense of collaboration and shared responsibility for security.

The design of a rewards program should be inclusive and accessible to all employees, regardless of their role or seniority. The criteria for rewards should be clear, transparent, and easily understood. Avoid overly complex or subjective criteria that might lead to perceived unfairness. Clear guidelines outlining the types of behaviors that are rewarded (e.g., reporting phishing attempts, attending security training, suggesting security improvements) will ensure consistency and fairness.

Consider establishing a tiered reward system, with different levels of recognition for different levels of contribution. This allows for a broader range of participation and ensures that even small contributions are acknowledged and appreciated. The rewards themselves can also vary, ranging from simple verbal praise to more substantial incentives such as gift cards, extra vacation days, or opportunities for professional development.

Integrating the rewards program into the existing performance review system can also enhance its effectiveness. Including security awareness and contributions as a specific performance metric can incentivize employees to prioritize security in their daily work. This approach not only promotes a culture of security but also aligns security performance with overall job performance, ensuring it's taken seriously.

Regular communication about the rewards program is crucial for its success. Regularly remind employees about the program, highlight recent winners, and showcase the positive impact of their contributions to the organization's security posture. This ongoing communication helps maintain momentum and ensures that the program remains top-of-mind for employees.

In addition to individual rewards, consider recognizing teams or departments that consistently demonstrate strong security practices. This team-based approach can foster a collaborative environment where security is viewed as a shared responsibility. For instance, a department that consistently achieves high compliance rates in security audits could be rewarded with a team lunch or a special event.

Measuring the effectiveness of the rewards program is equally important. Track the participation rates in the program, the types of rewards employees find most motivating, and the overall impact of the program on security incidents. This data can inform future iterations of the program, ensuring it continues to be effective and engaging. Analyzing the types of security incidents reported before and after the implementation of the rewards program can also be invaluable in assessing its impact.

The success of a rewards program hinges on its alignment with the overall organizational culture. If the culture values teamwork and collaboration, the rewards program should reflect those values. If the culture emphasizes individual achievement, the rewards program should acknowledge individual contributions. A properly designed and implemented rewards program fosters a sense of shared responsibility for security, encourages proactive security behaviors, and ultimately strengthens the organization's overall security posture. It's an investment that pays dividends in terms of a more secure and resilient workplace. This approach builds upon the foundation established in previous chapters by actively engaging employees and reinforcing the importance of cybersecurity within the organization. By making security a shared responsibility and acknowledging individual and team contributions, organizations create a virtuous cycle that enhances overall security and cultivates a stronger, more resilient security culture. The combination of training, communication, and a rewarding system ensures that security awareness isn't just a program, but a deeply ingrained organizational value. This comprehensive approach demonstrates the organization's commitment to security, fostering trust and empowering employees to become active participants in protecting sensitive information and maintaining a safe and secure work environment. Furthermore, by incorporating feedback from the rewards program itself, organizations can continuously improve and refine their approach, making it even more effective over time. This iterative process ensures that the program remains relevant and engaging, keeping employees involved and motivated to contribute to the organization's security. The ongoing evaluation and improvement are crucial for long-term success, creating a dynamic and evolving system that adapts to changing threats and organizational needs. This continuous feedback loop closes the circle, connecting employee contributions directly to organizational security improvements, creating a demonstrable ROI on the investment in security awareness. This tangible link strengthens the connection between individual actions and the organization's overall security posture, making the effort and participation even more meaningful. Finally, a key aspect that often gets overlooked is the public acknowledgment of employee contributions. This can significantly increase engagement and inspire others. Whether through internal newsletters, company-wide emails, or even a dedicated awards ceremony, recognizing employees publicly strengthens the culture of security and makes security a visible priority for all. This kind of recognition not only celebrates achievements but also implicitly encourages others to follow suit, creating a positive feedback loop where proactive security behaviors are rewarded and widely celebrated.

Addressing Security Incidents and Learning from Mistakes

Building upon the foundation of a robust rewards program and a culture of shared responsibility, the next crucial element in creating a truly effective cybersecurity awareness program is the proactive management and analysis of security incidents. While no organization can completely eliminate the risk of security breaches, how those incidents are handled significantly impacts the overall security posture and the effectiveness of future awareness initiatives. The key lies not in merely reacting to incidents, but in using them as powerful learning opportunities to refine existing processes, improve training, and reinforce the importance of security best practices.

The first critical step in addressing a security incident is swift and decisive action. A well-defined incident response plan, regularly tested and updated, is paramount. This plan should outline clear roles and responsibilities, escalation procedures, and communication protocols. It should also include detailed steps for containment, eradication, recovery, and post-incident analysis. The speed of response directly impacts the extent of the damage; the faster the organization can contain a breach, the less the potential for significant financial loss, reputational harm, and legal repercussions. This underscores the importance of regular security awareness training that equips employees with the knowledge to recognize suspicious activities and report them immediately.

Effective communication during and after a security incident is critical. Transparency, while adhering to legal and regulatory requirements, builds trust and demonstrates the organization's commitment to its employees and stakeholders. Regular updates, even if they contain limited information initially, keep everyone informed and prevent the spread of misinformation or rumors. This open communication fosters a collaborative environment, where employees feel empowered to report potential issues without fear of retribution. It is important to remember that even well-intentioned employees can inadvertently contribute to security vulnerabilities. Open communication minimizes blame and fosters a culture of learning from mistakes.

Post-incident analysis is perhaps the most crucial step. A thorough investigation should delve into the root cause of the incident, identifying the vulnerabilities exploited and the steps that led to the breach. This analysis should not just focus on technical vulnerabilities but also on human error, such as clicking on malicious links or falling for phishing scams. This is where the insights gleaned from the incident can significantly improve the organization's cybersecurity awareness program. For example, if a phishing attack proves successful due to a lack of employee awareness of sophisticated phishing techniques, the organization can update training materials to include more realistic and challenging simulations. If the incident reveals a weakness in the organization's security protocols, those protocols should be immediately revised and enhanced. This iterative process of improvement is a critical component of continuous security enhancement.

The post-incident analysis should not just be a technical exercise; it should also involve a review of the organization's security culture. Did employees feel empowered to report potential issues? Were communication channels effective? Were appropriate rewards and recognition offered for those who identified or helped to resolve the incident? These insights can inform improvements in communication strategies, employee engagement tactics, and the overall approach to building a culture of security. The process of analyzing the incident and identifying areas for improvement should be transparent and collaborative, involving representatives from different departments and levels of the organization. This inclusive approach not only identifies more potential areas for improvement but also fosters a stronger sense of shared responsibility for security.

Consider a scenario where a successful phishing attack resulted in a data breach. A thorough post-incident analysis might reveal that employees lacked sufficient training in identifying sophisticated phishing emails. This incident highlights a gap in the existing cybersecurity awareness program. The organization can then revise its training materials, incorporating more realistic phishing simulations and emphasizing techniques for identifying malicious emails. Furthermore, they might implement a new system for reporting suspicious emails, ensuring quicker response times. The incident provides valuable data for refining the training program, making it more relevant and effective. This iterative process ensures that the organization's security awareness program continues to evolve and adapt to ever-changing threats.

Another example could be an incident caused by an employee inadvertently downloading malware through an unsecured website. The post-incident analysis could reveal weaknesses in the organization's security policies regarding software downloads or a lack of awareness about safe browsing practices among employees. This would then lead to the implementation of stricter security policies, employee training on safe browsing habits, and the use of endpoint detection and response (EDR) solutions. The findings from the incident directly inform the necessary improvements and adjustments to the security program, minimizing the risk of similar incidents occurring in the future.

The importance of learning from mistakes cannot be overstated. Organizations should create a safe space where employees feel comfortable reporting incidents without fear of blame or punishment. This culture of transparency allows for a more comprehensive understanding of security vulnerabilities and enhances the effectiveness of corrective actions. Regularly reviewing incident reports and incorporating lessons learned into future training programs, policies, and procedures will significantly improve the organization's overall security posture over time. This continuous improvement cycle is crucial for staying ahead of evolving threats and building a resilient security culture.

Furthermore, the lessons learned from security incidents should be shared broadly within the organization. This could involve internal newsletters, presentations, or workshops. This broader dissemination of knowledge helps to reinforce security awareness across the entire workforce and encourages proactive security behaviors. This reinforces the message that security is a shared responsibility and that everyone plays a crucial role in protecting the organization's assets. By transforming security incidents from negative events into valuable learning experiences, organizations can significantly strengthen their cybersecurity posture and create a more secure and resilient work environment.

Finally, the entire process of incident response and post-incident analysis should be documented and regularly reviewed. This documentation serves not only as a record of past events but also as a valuable resource for continuous improvement. The lessons learned should be incorporated into the organization's security awareness program, ensuring that the program remains dynamic, relevant, and effective in protecting the organization against evolving threats. This continuous cycle of learning, improvement, and adaptation is crucial for building and maintaining a strong security culture within any organization. A comprehensive approach to security incident response and post-incident analysis transforms potential setbacks into opportunities for growth and strengthens the overall security posture. By fostering a culture of learning from mistakes, organizations build a more robust and resilient defense against future threats, making security not merely a program, but a deeply ingrained organizational value.

Creating a Continuous Improvement Cycle for Security Awareness

The success of any cybersecurity awareness program hinges on its ability to adapt and evolve. A static program, relying on the same materials and methods year after year, will quickly become ineffective as threats change and employee understanding stagnates. Therefore, establishing a continuous improvement cycle is paramount. This cycle isn't a one-time project; it's an ongoing process of assessment, refinement, and enhancement, ensuring the program remains relevant, engaging, and effective in protecting the organization's assets. This continuous cycle involves a series of steps, each building upon the previous one to create a dynamic and responsive security awareness culture.

The first step is rigorous
evaluation
. Simply delivering training and hoping for the best isn't enough. We need to systematically measure the effectiveness of our efforts. Kirkpatrick's Four Levels of Evaluation provide a robust framework for this. Level 1, Reaction, assesses participants' immediate responses to the training – did they find it engaging, relevant, and useful? Level 2, Learning, measures whether participants acquired the knowledge and skills imparted in the training. This can be assessed through quizzes, tests, or practical exercises. Level 3, Behavior, focuses on whether participants are actually applying the learned knowledge in their daily work. This often requires observation, analysis of security logs, or feedback from supervisors. Finally, Level 4, Results, assesses the overall impact of the training on the organization's security posture – a reduction in phishing attempts, fewer security incidents, or improved incident response times.

Employing a variety of evaluation methods is key to obtaining a holistic view. Surveys can capture employee feedback on the training materials and delivery methods. Analyzing security logs can reveal changes in user behavior after training. Regular phishing simulations provide a realistic assessment of employees' ability to identify and report suspicious emails. Comparing pre- and post-training data on incidents like password breaches or malware infections allows for a quantitative assessment of the program's impact. These multifaceted evaluations provide crucial insights into the strengths and weaknesses of the awareness program.

Once evaluation data is collected, the next phase is **analysis**. This involves carefully examining the results from different evaluation methods to identify areas for improvement. A low reaction score might indicate that the training materials are boring or irrelevant. Poor learning scores could suggest that the training content is too complex or poorly delivered. If behavior hasn't changed, it may mean that the training hasn't effectively translated into practical actions. Finally, a lack of positive results may point towards a need for program redesign or a focus on different areas. This analysis should be thorough, objective, and data-driven, providing a clear picture of where the program is succeeding and where it needs improvement.

The analysis should not only pinpoint weaknesses but also identify what aspects of the program were particularly successful. This positive reinforcement helps to maintain momentum and build confidence in the program's overall effectiveness. For example, if a particular phishing simulation proved highly successful in identifying vulnerabilities, the team can replicate the successful elements in future simulations or adapt those successful strategies into other training modules.

Based on this analysis, the third step is
improvement
. This involves making specific, actionable changes to the
awareness program to address the identified shortcomings.
For instance, if employee feedback reveals a lack of
engagement with e-learning modules, consider incorporating
gamification elements, interactive exercises, or shorter, more
frequent training sessions. If phishing simulation results
indicate a significant number of employees falling for
specific types of phishing attempts, update training materials
to address those specific techniques and tactics. If the
analysis points to a knowledge gap in a particular area, create
new training modules to address that specific topic.
The improvements should be carefully planned and
implemented, with clear goals and metrics in place to
measure their effectiveness.

Moreover, it's crucial to adapt to the evolving threat
landscape. Cybersecurity threats are constantly evolving,
with new tactics and techniques emerging regularly.
Therefore, the awareness program must be dynamic enough
to reflect these changes. Regularly update training materials
to reflect the latest threats, vulnerabilities, and best practices.
Introduce new training modules to address emerging threats
as they appear. Stay informed about the latest security news
and trends and adjust the program accordingly. Collaboration
with internal security teams, participation in industry
conferences and workshops, and engagement with external
security experts are crucial in staying abreast of the latest
advancements and trends.

The final step is
documentation and communication
.
Detailed records of the evaluation, analysis, and
improvement processes should be maintained. This
documentation serves as a valuable resource for future
improvements, providing a historical record of the program's

evolution and the effectiveness of various interventions. This documentation should clearly outline the methodologies used, data collected, analysis performed, and improvements implemented. This documented history allows for better informed decisions and a deeper understanding of the long-term impact of different strategies. Moreover, this transparency builds trust and credibility within the organization, demonstrating a commitment to continuous improvement.

Regularly communicate the results of the improvement cycle to stakeholders, including senior management, employees, and the security team. Highlighting successes, challenges, and plans for future improvements promotes accountability and keeps everyone informed about the program's progress. This communication can take the form of regular reports, presentations, or informal updates. This continuous feedback loop ensures buy-in from all levels of the organization and strengthens the overall commitment to cybersecurity awareness.

This cyclical approach – evaluation, analysis, improvement, and documentation – is not a linear process; it's iterative. The results from one cycle inform the next, constantly refining and enhancing the awareness program. By embracing this continuous improvement model, organizations can build a robust and adaptable cybersecurity awareness program that effectively protects their assets and fosters a culture of security throughout the organization. This isn't just about compliance or ticking boxes; it's about building a proactive and resilient security culture, where employees are empowered to identify and respond to threats effectively, ultimately minimizing the organization's risk profile.

The key to long-term success lies in building a feedback mechanism that is easily accessible and encourages employee participation. This could involve anonymous surveys, suggestion boxes, or regular feedback sessions. Actively seeking employee input ensures that the training remains relevant to their experiences and challenges. A program that genuinely listens to its audience is much more likely to foster buy-in and achieve lasting improvements. Regularly reviewing and updating the program ensures it stays current with the ever-evolving threat landscape and reflects changes in employee roles and responsibilities.

Furthermore, the program's success hinges on effective communication. It's not enough to simply roll out training; employees need to be regularly reminded of the importance of cybersecurity and engaged with new and relevant information. This necessitates a multi-faceted approach, utilizing various channels such as email newsletters, posters, internal websites, and even short, engaging videos. Regular reminders, coupled with real-world examples of security breaches and their consequences, can dramatically increase employee awareness and vigilance.

Finally, consider the importance of leadership buy-in. If senior management isn't demonstrably committed to cybersecurity awareness, it's difficult to expect employees to take it seriously. Senior leaders should actively participate in the program, endorsing its importance and setting an example for others to follow. This visible commitment helps establish a strong security culture where cybersecurity isn't viewed as a separate entity but as an integral part of the organization's overall strategy. By consistently promoting a culture of security awareness, emphasizing its importance, and demonstrating a genuine commitment to continuous improvement, organizations can significantly reduce their risk profile and build a stronger, more resilient security posture. This proactive approach not only minimizes the impact of security incidents but also strengthens the organization's overall operational effectiveness and enhances its reputation.

Implementing Advanced Phishing Simulations

Implementing sophisticated phishing simulations represents a critical advancement in cybersecurity awareness training. Moving beyond basic, generic phishing campaigns, advanced simulations mirror real-world attacks, offering a far more realistic and effective evaluation of employee vulnerability. This necessitates a shift in approach, requiring a deeper understanding of attacker methodologies and the ability to tailor simulations to the specific context of the target organization.

Spear phishing, a highly targeted form of phishing, is a prime example. Unlike generic phishing emails sent indiscriminately to a large group, spear phishing campaigns meticulously research individual targets, tailoring the message to their specific roles, responsibilities, and interests. This personalization dramatically increases the likelihood of success, as the email appears legitimate and relevant to the recipient. For instance, a spear phishing attack might target a finance department employee with an email seemingly from the CEO, requesting urgent wire transfer of funds. The email's language, tone, and even the sender's email address might be subtly crafted to evade suspicion. Simulating such attacks allows organizations to assess the effectiveness of their security awareness training in combating these highly targeted and potentially devastating threats. Successful simulation designs will require in-depth knowledge of the target's communication networks, social media activity and even public record information to effectively craft believable personas and email content.

Whaling, an even more advanced form of spear phishing, specifically targets high-profile individuals within an organization, such as CEOs, CFOs, or other executives. These individuals often handle sensitive information and financial transactions, making them particularly attractive targets. Whaling attacks typically involve extensive research to understand the target's communication patterns, relationships, and decision-making processes. The attackers often use sophisticated techniques to build trust and urgency, creating a sense of legitimacy that encourages the target to take action without verifying the authenticity of the request. Simulating whaling attacks requires meticulous planning and execution, ensuring that the simulation closely replicates the nuances of a real-world attack. A carefully crafted email from what seems to be a trusted business associate requesting immediate action, or a phone call that mirrors a known associate's communication style, can test whether upper management are susceptible to such an attack. Furthermore, post-simulation analysis of how upper management acted is crucial, showing gaps in their understanding of these threats and allowing for adjustment to training procedures.

The design and implementation of advanced phishing simulations necessitate a multi-faceted approach. First, meticulous planning is crucial. This involves identifying key personnel and departments most susceptible to specific attack vectors. Understanding the organization's internal structure, communication flows, and existing security protocols is critical. The simulations should be designed to assess the effectiveness of existing security controls, not just employee awareness. For example, is there a policy that would alert senior management to any large transaction that needs to be approved? Is there a verification procedure for requests of this kind? Testing these parameters in tandem with employee awareness helps assess the totality of vulnerability.

Secondly, the creation of realistic and convincing phishing emails or other attack vectors is paramount. This requires not only crafting believable content but also replicating the technical characteristics of authentic communications. For example, spoofing email addresses and employing techniques to bypass spam filters can make the simulation more realistic. Even the incorporation of subtly flawed elements into the mock emails – a misplaced logo, incorrect grammar, or unexpected links – can allow assessment of employee attention to detail and critical thinking skills during training.

Thirdly, robust data collection and analysis are essential. The simulation should track not only the success rate of the attack but also the specific actions taken by each employee. This data can be used to identify areas of weakness in employee training, pinpoint vulnerable departments, and inform the development of targeted training materials. Data analysis should extend beyond simply identifying who fell for the scam. The analysis should explore
why
they fell for the scam – did they open a suspicious attachment? Did they fail to verify the sender's identity? Such insight allows for a more focused approach to future training initiatives.
Anonymous surveys post-simulation can help gather insights into what employees struggled with during the simulation and what they found particularly compelling or suspicious about the attacks. This valuable data allows for a more personalized approach to future training.

Finally, the results of the simulation must be communicated effectively to employees. This is not just about highlighting who failed but also about reinforcing the importance of security awareness. The debrief should focus on lessons learned and provide actionable advice to improve individual security practices. Transparency is key: explaining the rationale behind the simulation and how the data will be used to improve the overall security posture of the organization can foster a more collaborative and security-conscious culture. It is a chance to show employees that the simulations aren't just tests but valuable learning opportunities.

The integration of advanced phishing simulations with other security awareness initiatives is crucial for maximizing their impact. For example, the simulation could be combined with e-learning modules, classroom training, or awareness campaigns to reinforce key security concepts and provide consistent messaging. This approach allows employees to learn from their mistakes in a safe environment, without facing real-world consequences. The focus should be not just on pointing out mistakes, but rather on a thorough understanding of the 'why' behind the attack. The training should also discuss the long-term impacts of phishing and similar attacks – damage to reputation, financial costs, legal issues. This helps foster a deeper appreciation for the importance of strong security practices.

Furthermore, regular and varied phishing simulations, using different techniques and scenarios, are critical to maintaining a high level of security awareness. Employees' vigilance can wane over time if simulations become predictable. The introduction of unexpected simulation methods – SMS phishing (smishing), voicemail phishing (vishing) – will provide employees with exposure to the wide range of threats they could encounter in the real world. The frequency of simulations should also be considered, allowing for an ongoing and relevant learning process for employees. Over-simulating can lead to employee fatigue and reduce the overall effectiveness of the program, whereas infrequent simulations can lead to a decreased vigilance amongst staff.

Advanced phishing simulations are not a standalone solution for ensuring cybersecurity awareness. They are a powerful tool that, when integrated within a comprehensive security awareness program, can significantly improve an organization's overall security posture. By combining realistic simulations with effective training materials, consistent messaging, and ongoing reinforcement, organizations can effectively equip their workforce to withstand even the most sophisticated cyber threats. The key is to treat the simulations as a valuable learning opportunity rather than a mere test, fostering a culture of continuous learning and improvement in cybersecurity awareness. Through regular review and adjustment of methodologies, a more secure organization can be fostered through employee education and a continual refinement of training.

Utilizing Security Awareness Platforms and Tools

The effectiveness of a robust cybersecurity awareness program hinges not only on the quality of its content and delivery methods but also on the tools and platforms used to manage and deliver that training. The market offers a wide array of security awareness platforms, each with unique features, capabilities, and pricing models. Selecting the right platform is crucial, as it will significantly impact the program's reach, engagement, and overall success. This choice depends heavily on the specific needs and resources of the organization. Factors such as the size of the workforce, budget constraints, existing IT infrastructure, and desired level of sophistication in training delivery must be carefully considered.

A critical aspect to examine is the platform's ability to deliver engaging and relevant training content. Many platforms offer pre-built modules covering common cybersecurity threats, such as phishing, malware, and social engineering. However, the best platforms allow for customization, enabling organizations to tailor training to their specific industry, organizational culture, and the types of threats they face. This customization ensures that the training is relevant and resonates with employees, increasing engagement and knowledge retention. Look for platforms that offer a diverse range of content formats, including interactive modules, videos, simulations, and gamified challenges. This variety caters to different learning styles and keeps employees engaged.

Beyond content delivery, the platform's reporting and analytics capabilities are crucial for measuring the effectiveness of the training program. A strong platform should provide detailed reports on employee participation, performance on assessments, and overall program impact. This data is essential for identifying areas for improvement and demonstrating the ROI of the awareness program. Look for platforms that offer comprehensive reporting features, allowing you to track key metrics such as completion rates, quiz scores, and user engagement. These metrics, aligned with Kirkpatrick's Four Levels of Evaluation (reaction, learning, behavior, results), paint a holistic picture of the program's success. The ability to segment data by department, location, or job role offers valuable insights into the effectiveness of the program across various groups within the organization.

Another crucial element to consider is the platform's integration capabilities. A well-designed platform should seamlessly integrate with existing IT infrastructure and other security tools. This integration minimizes disruptions and simplifies program management. For example, the platform should ideally integrate with the organization's identity and access management (IAM) system, allowing for automated user provisioning and de-provisioning. Integration with learning management systems (LMS) can streamline the administration of training and provide a central repository for all employee training records. Furthermore, integration with security information and event management (SIEM) systems can provide real-time threat intelligence, enriching the training content and making it more relevant to current threats.

Scalability is another essential feature. As the organization grows, the platform should be able to accommodate the increasing number of users and training needs without sacrificing performance or functionality. Consider whether the platform offers flexible pricing plans that can scale with the organization's growth. A platform that lacks scalability may become a bottleneck in the future, limiting the effectiveness of the awareness program. Organizations should also examine the platform's support capabilities. Look for a vendor that offers responsive and reliable technical support, readily accessible documentation, and regular software updates. Effective support is crucial for ensuring that the platform remains operational and performs optimally.

The user interface (UI) and user experience (UX) are often overlooked but are crucial for ensuring that employees readily adopt and use the platform. A user-friendly interface makes training accessible and engaging, encouraging employees to participate actively. A complicated or clunky interface can lead to frustration and decreased participation, undermining the program's effectiveness. Prioritize platforms with intuitive interfaces and easy-to-navigate features, making it easy for employees to access training materials and complete assessments.

Beyond the core functionalities, consider the vendor's reputation and their commitment to innovation. A reputable vendor will have a track record of delivering reliable and effective solutions. Look for vendors that invest in research and development, continually updating their platforms with new features and content to stay ahead of the evolving threat landscape. Reading customer reviews and testimonials can provide valuable insights into the vendor's reputation and the quality of their support. Choosing a vendor committed to continuous improvement ensures that the awareness program remains current and effective.

Let's explore some specific examples of security awareness platforms to illustrate the diversity available. Some platforms, like KnowBe4, are well-known for their comprehensive phishing simulations and engaging training modules. They excel at providing realistic scenarios that test employee response to sophisticated phishing attempts. However, their focus on simulations might mean a less comprehensive approach to other crucial aspects of security awareness training.

Other platforms, such as Proofpoint, offer a broader range of features, including email security, incident response, and security awareness training. Their integrated approach can streamline security operations, but might come at a higher cost and potentially with more complexity in implementation. Finally, smaller, more specialized platforms may focus on niche areas, such as secure coding practices or specific industry regulations. These platforms often offer highly tailored content but might lack the breadth of features found in larger, more comprehensive solutions.

The selection process should not be driven solely by price. While budget is a vital consideration, it shouldn't overshadow the platform's ability to meet the organization's specific needs and deliver measurable results. Investing in a robust platform that effectively addresses the organization's vulnerabilities is far more cost-effective than dealing with the consequences of a successful cyberattack. Furthermore, a cost-benefit analysis, carefully considering the potential losses from a breach compared to the cost of the platform, can help justify the investment to stakeholders.

The choice of platform should be aligned with the organization's overall security strategy. It should integrate seamlessly with existing security controls and enhance the effectiveness of other security initiatives. The platform should not exist in isolation but should be a key component of a holistic security awareness program, encompassing regular communication, employee feedback mechanisms, and ongoing reinforcement of key security practices.

Regularly reviewing and updating the platform's content and features is crucial to maintain its effectiveness against evolving cyber threats. Consider incorporating employee feedback into the selection process, ensuring the platform resonates with the users and encourages participation.

In conclusion, selecting the right security awareness platform is a multifaceted decision. It requires a thorough assessment of the organization's needs, resources, and existing infrastructure. By carefully evaluating the features, functionalities, and capabilities of various platforms, organizations can select a solution that effectively delivers engaging and impactful cybersecurity awareness training, ultimately strengthening their overall security posture. The chosen platform should be more than just a tool; it should be a strategic investment in protecting the organization's valuable assets and ensuring the long-term security of its operations. The iterative nature of cybersecurity necessitates a continuous review of the platform's effectiveness and a willingness to adapt and update the program based on evolving threats and technological advancements. Regular audits and performance evaluations are critical to ensure the platform continues to align with the organization's evolving security objectives.

Integrating Security Awareness into DevOps and Agile Methodologies

The seamless integration of security awareness into the rapid-paced environments of DevOps and Agile methodologies presents a unique challenge. Traditional, static security training programs simply cannot keep pace with the iterative nature of these development models. The constant updates, deployments, and feedback loops demand a more dynamic and integrated approach to security awareness. Instead of viewing security as a separate phase, it must become an inherent part of every stage of the software development lifecycle (SDLC). This requires a shift in mindset, from treating security as an afterthought to embedding it proactively throughout the entire process.

One key aspect of this integration is the adoption of "Security Champions" within development teams. These individuals, selected for their technical expertise and influence within the team, act as advocates for security best practices. They are not necessarily security experts, but rather individuals who understand the development process and can effectively communicate security concerns and best practices to their colleagues. Their role involves actively participating in code reviews, identifying potential vulnerabilities, and promoting secure coding practices within the team. Training these champions is crucial; they need a deep understanding of the security risks relevant to their specific projects and the tools and techniques to mitigate those risks. This training should not be a one-time event but an ongoing process, keeping them up-to-date with the latest threats and vulnerabilities. Regular refresher training, access to online resources, and opportunities for knowledge sharing with other security champions across the organization are essential.

Furthermore, integrating security awareness into the daily routines of developers necessitates incorporating security into the tools and technologies used in DevOps and Agile. This can involve integrating security scanning tools into the Continuous Integration/Continuous Delivery (CI/CD) pipeline. These automated tools can scan code for vulnerabilities during the development process, identifying and reporting potential issues before they reach production. This proactive approach significantly reduces the risk of deploying vulnerable software, saving time and resources in the long run. The results of these scans should be readily accessible to developers, and ideally incorporated into the team's dashboards, providing immediate feedback and encouraging rapid remediation. This seamless integration ensures that security is not treated as an isolated concern but is actively addressed throughout the development pipeline. The culture needs to support the timely remediation of security flaws, not penalize developers for discovering them.

Beyond automated tools, interactive training modules can be integrated directly into the development workflow. These modules can provide targeted training on specific security risks and best practices relevant to the current project. For example, a module might focus on securing APIs, preventing SQL injection attacks, or handling sensitive data appropriately. These modules should be short, engaging, and relevant to the developer's immediate work, rather than lengthy theoretical lectures. Microlearning techniques, such as short videos and interactive quizzes, are particularly effective in this context. The focus should be on practical application and reinforcement of key concepts through real-world examples. The use of gamification techniques, leaderboards, and reward systems can further enhance engagement and motivation.

Agile methodologies, with their iterative approach and emphasis on collaboration, present unique opportunities for integrating security awareness. Security considerations should be integrated into sprint planning and retrospectives. During sprint planning, the team can identify potential security risks associated with the planned features and incorporate appropriate mitigations into the sprint backlog. During retrospectives, the team can review the security aspects of the completed sprint, identifying areas for improvement and incorporating those lessons into future sprints. This iterative approach ensures that security is continuously evaluated and improved throughout the project lifecycle. It's vital to involve security personnel in these discussions, but their role should be collaborative and supportive, not dictatorial.

The use of secure coding guidelines and style guides is also critical. These documents provide developers with clear instructions on how to write secure code, covering common vulnerabilities and best practices. These guidelines should be easily accessible and integrated into the development environment, perhaps even incorporated into the IDE's automated code completion features. Regular training on these guidelines ensures that developers are aware of the standards and encouraged to follow them consistently.

Finally, the importance of security awareness training in the context of DevOps and Agile extends beyond the development team itself. It must also encompass operations, IT, and security personnel. Collaboration and communication between these teams is essential to ensure that security is effectively addressed throughout the entire software delivery pipeline. Cross-training initiatives can facilitate this collaboration, enabling individuals from different teams to understand each other's roles and responsibilities and work together more effectively. Regular meetings and knowledge-sharing sessions can further foster communication and ensure that everyone is on the same page.

The effectiveness of these integrated approaches must be continuously monitored and evaluated. Regular security assessments, penetration testing, and vulnerability scans can help identify areas for improvement in the security awareness program. The feedback from these assessments should be used to refine the training materials and processes, ensuring that the program remains relevant and effective. This continuous feedback loop ensures the program adapts to the ever-evolving threat landscape and the changing needs of the development process. It's not enough to simply implement these strategies; they must be nurtured and adapted over time.

The successful integration of security awareness into DevOps and Agile methodologies requires a cultural shift within the organization. Security should not be viewed as a separate function but as a shared responsibility. By fostering a culture of security awareness and collaboration, organizations can effectively mitigate the risks associated with rapid development cycles and enhance the overall security posture of their software applications. This involves a conscious effort to make security training relevant, engaging, and easily accessible to developers working under pressure to deliver software quickly. This requires investment in the right tools and resources, but the potential payoff – more secure software, fewer vulnerabilities, and reduced risk – is significant. The constant iteration of Agile and DevOps requires a similarly iterative approach to security training and awareness; it's a continuous process, not a one-time project. The long-term benefits of this approach significantly outweigh the initial investment in both time and resources. Organizations adopting this integrated strategy will be better positioned to respond effectively to evolving threats and maintain a strong security posture in the face of ever-increasing complexity. The goal isn't just compliance; it's building a culture where security is considered fundamental to the development process, from inception to deployment and beyond. This proactive approach transforms security from a potential bottleneck into a key enabler of faster, more secure software delivery.

The Role of Artificial Intelligence in Cybersecurity Awareness

The integration of artificial intelligence (AI) into cybersecurity awareness training represents a significant leap forward in effectiveness and personalization. Traditional methods, while valuable, often suffer from a lack of individual tailoring, leading to disengagement and reduced knowledge retention. AI offers a solution by analyzing individual learning styles, identifying knowledge gaps, and dynamically adjusting training content to maximize impact. This personalized approach can significantly improve the effectiveness of awareness programs, leading to a more informed and security-conscious workforce.

One key application of AI lies in adaptive learning platforms. These platforms use algorithms to track a user's progress, identifying areas where they struggle and adapting the training accordingly. Instead of presenting a one-size-fits-all curriculum, the AI tailors the content to the individual's specific needs and pace. For instance, an employee who demonstrates difficulty understanding phishing techniques will receive more focused training on that topic, while another employee who already possesses strong knowledge in this area can move on to more advanced concepts. This dynamic adaptation ensures that training time is used efficiently and that employees gain the specific knowledge required to navigate the ever-evolving landscape of cyber threats.

Furthermore, AI-powered systems can analyze vast datasets of cybersecurity incidents and threats to identify emerging trends and patterns. This allows for the creation of more relevant and timely training modules that address current vulnerabilities and attack vectors. Traditional training programs often lag behind the rapid pace of technological advancement and the evolution of cyber threats. AI helps bridge this gap by providing real-time insights and enabling the rapid development of targeted training materials. This ensures that employees are equipped with the most up-to-date knowledge and skills necessary to protect the organization from the latest threats.

Beyond adaptive learning, AI can significantly enhance the engagement and interactivity of cybersecurity awareness training. AI-powered chatbots can simulate realistic phishing attempts, allowing employees to practice identifying and responding to these attacks in a safe and controlled environment. These interactive simulations are far more engaging than traditional lectures or reading materials, leading to improved knowledge retention and practical skills development. The chatbot can provide immediate feedback, explaining why a particular action was correct or incorrect, reinforcing learning and solidifying understanding. This interactive approach fosters a more active and participatory learning experience, improving the overall effectiveness of the training.

AI can also be leveraged to create more personalized phishing simulations. Rather than sending generic phishing emails to all employees, AI can analyze individual user profiles and behaviors to create targeted attacks tailored to their specific vulnerabilities. For example, an employee who frequently accesses social media accounts might receive a phishing email disguised as a notification from a social media platform. This personalized approach increases the likelihood of successfully identifying vulnerabilities and improving individual awareness. By focusing on specific individual risk factors, the AI can help close gaps in the organization's security posture.

Another exciting application of AI is in the development of automated feedback mechanisms. Instead of relying on manual review of training completion and assessments, AI can automate the process, providing instant feedback to employees and tracking their progress in real time. This allows for a more timely and efficient assessment of the training's effectiveness. The automation reduces the burden on training administrators and enables them to focus on refining the training program and developing new content. AI can even analyze employee responses to identify patterns of misunderstanding or confusion, providing insights into areas where the training needs improvement. This data-driven approach leads to continual program refinement and improved training efficacy.

However, the implementation of AI in cybersecurity awareness training is not without challenges. Data privacy concerns are paramount, as AI systems require access to employee data to personalize training and assess its effectiveness. It's crucial to ensure that data is collected, processed, and stored in accordance with relevant privacy regulations and best practices. Transparency with employees about data usage is vital to build trust and maintain confidence in the program.

Another challenge is the potential for bias in AI algorithms. If the training data reflects existing biases, the AI may perpetuate these biases in its recommendations and assessments. It is essential to carefully curate the training data and regularly audit the AI algorithms to ensure fairness and prevent the perpetuation of harmful stereotypes. The goal is to create an inclusive and equitable training program that benefits all employees, regardless of background or experience.

The cost of implementing AI-powered cybersecurity awareness training can also be a barrier for some organizations. The development and maintenance of sophisticated AI systems require significant investment in infrastructure, software, and expertise. However, the long-term benefits of improved security awareness and reduced risk often outweigh the initial investment. Organizations should carefully consider their budget and resources before committing to an AI-powered solution.

Moreover, the effectiveness of AI in cybersecurity awareness training is dependent on the quality of the data used to train the algorithms. If the data is inaccurate, incomplete, or biased, the AI will produce unreliable results. Therefore, it is crucial to invest in high-quality data collection and preprocessing techniques. Regular data validation and monitoring are essential to ensure the accuracy and reliability of the AI system. Only with accurate, well-curated data can the AI system truly optimize and personalize training effectively.

In conclusion, AI has the potential to revolutionize cybersecurity awareness training by providing personalized, engaging, and adaptive learning experiences. By leveraging AI's capabilities in adaptive learning, personalized phishing simulations, automated feedback, and data-driven insights, organizations can significantly improve the effectiveness of their awareness programs and cultivate a more security-conscious workforce. However, careful consideration must be given to data privacy, algorithmic bias, cost, and data quality to ensure the responsible and successful implementation of AI in this crucial area. The ongoing evolution of AI and its applications in cybersecurity will continue to reshape the landscape of security awareness training, offering ever-more sophisticated and effective methods to protect organizations from the ever-evolving threats of the digital age. Organizations that proactively embrace these technological advancements will be better positioned to mitigate cyber risks and build a more resilient security posture. The integration of AI represents a significant step forward in strengthening cybersecurity awareness and protecting the valuable assets of organizations in the face of increasingly sophisticated and persistent cyberattacks. This continuous adaptation to new technologies and approaches is essential for maintaining a robust and effective cybersecurity awareness program. Regular review and updates to the program, incorporating the latest AI advancements and best practices, are vital to ensuring its ongoing effectiveness and relevance.

Emerging Threats and Future Trends in Cybersecurity Awareness

The rapid evolution of cyber threats necessitates a continuous adaptation of cybersecurity awareness programs. What worked effectively last year might be obsolete today, highlighting the crucial need for ongoing learning and development within organizations. The threat landscape is dynamic, with new attack vectors emerging constantly. Understanding these emerging threats and anticipating future trends is paramount to maintaining a robust and effective security posture.

One significant emerging threat is the increasing sophistication of social engineering attacks. Phishing scams are no longer limited to crude attempts at impersonating legitimate entities. Attackers are employing highly personalized and targeted approaches, leveraging readily available personal information from social media and other online sources to craft convincing messages. These attacks often incorporate sophisticated techniques like spear phishing, whaling (targeting high-profile individuals), and quid pro quo scams, promising rewards or services in exchange for sensitive information. Cybersecurity awareness training must emphasize the ability to critically assess communications and identify the subtle indicators of malicious activity, regardless of how convincing the message may seem. This includes teaching employees to verify sender identities, examine email headers and links for anomalies, and understand the different forms social engineering can take. Regular phishing simulations, designed to mirror the complexity of real-world attacks, are vital for building employee resilience against these evolving threats.

Another key area of concern is the proliferation of ransomware attacks. These attacks are becoming more frequent and damaging, often targeting critical infrastructure and organizations with large amounts of sensitive data. Ransomware gangs are employing increasingly sophisticated techniques to encrypt data, demanding higher ransoms, and using double extortion tactics, threatening to publicly release stolen data if the ransom is not paid. Cybersecurity awareness programs need to educate employees about the risks associated with ransomware, emphasizing safe file-sharing practices, the importance of regular software updates and patching, and the necessity of backing up critical data. Moreover, employees must understand the company's response procedures in the event of a ransomware attack, ensuring a coordinated and effective response. Simulated ransomware attacks can effectively demonstrate the potential damage and underscore the importance of preventive measures.

The Internet of Things (IoT) presents a significant challenge to cybersecurity. The ever-increasing number of interconnected devices, many with limited security features, creates an expanded attack surface for cybercriminals. These devices can be compromised to launch attacks against other systems, act as entry points into networks, or be used to collect sensitive data. Cybersecurity awareness training must include education on the security implications of IoT devices, emphasizing safe practices for connecting and using these devices, understanding the potential risks, and reporting suspicious activity. This includes educating employees about the risks of using unsecure public Wi-Fi networks, downloading apps from unverified sources, and failing to update the firmware of their IoT devices.

Artificial Intelligence (AI) is being increasingly leveraged by both attackers and defenders. While AI can significantly enhance cybersecurity defenses by automating threat detection and response, it also presents new challenges. Attackers are using AI to automate the creation of sophisticated phishing emails, develop advanced malware, and launch highly targeted attacks. Cybersecurity awareness training needs to incorporate an understanding of the capabilities of AI in both offensive and defensive contexts, emphasizing the importance of human vigilance and critical thinking, even in the face of highly sophisticated attacks. Employees must understand that AI-powered tools can still be tricked or circumvented and the importance of human intervention in security decision-making processes remains crucial.

The rise of deepfakes presents another emerging threat. Deepfakes are synthetic media, such as videos and audio recordings, that appear realistic but are actually fabricated using advanced AI techniques. These deepfakes can be used for various malicious purposes, including spreading disinformation, damaging reputations, and conducting sophisticated social engineering attacks. Cybersecurity awareness programs should educate employees on how to identify deepfakes and their potential risks. This includes teaching them to be critical of online content, particularly videos and audio recordings that appear unusually convincing or make extraordinary claims, verifying information from multiple trusted sources, and understanding that deepfakes are becoming increasingly sophisticated, making detection more challenging.

Cloud computing, while offering numerous benefits, also introduces new security challenges. Organizations relying heavily on cloud services must ensure they have robust security measures in place to protect their data and systems.

Cybersecurity awareness training should cover the security aspects of cloud computing, emphasizing the shared responsibility model between the cloud provider and the organization, safe cloud usage practices, and the importance of data encryption and access control.

The increasing prevalence of mobile devices in the workplace poses further security risks. Employees often use personal devices for work, blurring the lines between personal and professional data security. Cybersecurity awareness training must address mobile device security, including the use of strong passwords, secure Wi-Fi networks, and up-to-date security software. Training should also include guidance on avoiding risky apps, understanding the risks associated with phishing attacks targeting mobile devices, and proper disposal of outdated or lost devices.

The future of cybersecurity awareness will undoubtedly involve more sophisticated training methods, incorporating gamification, virtual reality, and other immersive technologies to enhance engagement and retention. The focus will shift towards building a security-conscious culture, rather than just delivering rote information. This means fostering a collaborative environment where employees feel empowered to report security incidents and participate actively in maintaining a secure workplace. Continuous improvement and refinement of awareness programs based on data analysis and feedback are crucial. Tracking metrics, analyzing incident reports, and incorporating lessons learned into future training modules is essential for ensuring the ongoing effectiveness of cybersecurity awareness initiatives. Regular review and updates to the program, incorporating the latest threats and best practices, are vital to ensuring its ongoing effectiveness and relevance.

The evolution of cybersecurity awareness will also involve a stronger emphasis on human factors. While technological solutions are crucial, human error remains a significant factor in many cyber incidents. Therefore, training will need to focus more on developing critical thinking skills, enhancing situational awareness, and promoting a proactive security mindset. This will involve incorporating elements of psychology and behavioral science into training programs, to better understand and address human vulnerabilities.

The integration of advanced technologies like blockchain and quantum computing will impact both offensive and defensive cybersecurity strategies. Blockchain's potential for enhanced security and transparency needs to be explored and incorporated into training programs, while the potential threats of quantum computing to current encryption methods need to be acknowledged and addressed. Awareness training must evolve to reflect these advancements, ensuring that employees understand both the opportunities and challenges these technologies present.

In conclusion, emerging threats and future trends in cybersecurity highlight the importance of ongoing adaptation and continuous learning. Cybersecurity awareness programs must remain dynamic, incorporating the latest threats, technologies, and best practices to effectively protect organizations from the ever-evolving landscape of cyberattacks. Regular review, updating, and measurement of program effectiveness are vital to ensuring that organizations maintain a robust security posture and foster a culture of cybersecurity awareness among their employees. The investment in robust, adaptable, and engaging cybersecurity awareness training is not just a cost, but an essential component of a comprehensive cybersecurity strategy, ensuring the long-term protection of organizational assets and reputation. The future of cybersecurity awareness is not simply about imparting knowledge, but about cultivating a culture of vigilance, responsibility, and proactive security among all members of an organization. By embracing continuous learning and adaptation, organizations can significantly reduce their vulnerability to increasingly sophisticated cyber threats.

Acknowledgments

Writing a book is rarely a solitary endeavor, and this one is no exception. I extend my deepest gratitude to [List names and affiliations of individuals who provided significant contributions, e.g., reviewers, editors, colleagues, family members]. Your insights, feedback, and unwavering support were instrumental in shaping this book into its final form. Special thanks go to [Mention specific individuals and their contributions, e.g., "Dr. X for their invaluable expertise on Kirkpatrick's Four Levels," or "Y for their meticulous editing and patience"]. Your contributions are deeply appreciated. Finally, I acknowledge the countless cybersecurity professionals whose dedication and hard work inspired this project. This book is dedicated to them.

Appendix

This appendix contains supplementary materials to enhance your understanding and application of the concepts discussed in this book. Specifically, it includes:

Appendix A: Templates for Cybersecurity Awareness Materials:

This section provides downloadable templates for creating various cybersecurity awareness materials, including email templates, poster designs, quiz questions, and e-learning module outlines. These templates are designed to be easily customized to fit your specific organizational needs.

Appendix B: Glossary of Cybersecurity Terms:

A comprehensive glossary of key cybersecurity terms used throughout the book, providing clear and concise definitions for both technical and non-technical audiences.

Appendix C: Case Studies:

Detailed case studies illustrating successful cybersecurity awareness programs in various organizational settings. These case studies provide practical examples of how the strategies outlined in this book can be implemented effectively.

Appendix D: Further Reading and Resources:

A curated list of recommended resources for continued learning and professional development in the field of cybersecurity awareness. This includes links to relevant websites, articles, and publications.

Glossary

This glossary provides definitions for key terms used throughout the book. For more detailed explanations, refer to the relevant chapters.

Cybersecurity Awareness:
Understanding and practicing safe online behaviors to protect oneself and organizational assets from cyber threats.

Phishing:
A deceptive attempt to obtain sensitive information such as usernames, passwords, and credit card details by disguising as a trustworthy entity in electronic communication.

Social Engineering:
Manipulative techniques used to trick individuals into divulging confidential information or performing actions that compromise security.

Kirkpatrick's Four Levels of Evaluation:
A model for evaluating training programs that assesses reaction, learning, behavior, and results.

SMART Goals:
Specific, Measurable, Achievable, Relevant, and Time-bound goals.

Return on Investment (ROI):
A measure of the profitability of a cybersecurity awareness program, expressed as a ratio of gain to cost.

GDPR (General Data Protection Regulation):
A regulation in the European Union and the European Economic Area relating to data protection and privacy.

CCPA (California Consumer Privacy Act):
A state law in California relating to data protection and privacy.

[Add other relevant terms and definitions as needed]

References

[List all cited works using a consistent citation style, such as APA or MLA. Include full bibliographic information for each source.]

Author Biography

[Insert a brief biography of the author, highlighting their relevant experience and expertise in cybersecurity, training, and writing. Include information about their education, professional certifications, and any notable publications or achievements. For example:]

[Author Name] is a highly experienced Information Security Professional and Consultant with over [Number] years of experience in designing and implementing effective cybersecurity awareness programs for organizations of all sizes. They hold a [Degree] in [Field of Study] from [University] and possess several industry-recognized certifications, including [List Certifications]. [He/She/They] have a proven track record of success in reducing security incidents and improving organizational security postures through engaging and impactful training initiatives. [Author Name] is also a published author and frequent speaker at cybersecurity conferences. Their passion lies in making cybersecurity accessible and engaging for everyone, regardless of technical background.